ATHLETES PRESSING CHARGES

FIGHTING FOR THE FUTURE OF MODERN PENTATHLON

SHARP IDEAS

The book series "Sharp Ideas in Sport" is aimed to advance existing contemporary discussions on sport and body culture through providing critical debates and challenging perspectives. The series is established with the ambition to create a hub for controversial, radical, and provocative views that challenge current insights into global sport. The concise pocket book format allows the general public to access our books but equally informs academic debate.

The rationale for the series stems from a trend in academia and wider society that controversial thoughts and arguments are often neglected in favor of popular or uncontentious views. Books, academic articles, and contributions to anthologies on sensitive topics that have merit but are socially or ideologically offensive are often suppressed. Such moral culture in scholarly work threatens the academic freedom that is supposed to perpetuate the status quo in our societies and therewith the future of our university institutions.

"Sharp Ideas in Sport" provides a forum that is detached from mainstream political and ideological viewpoints, and open for anyone who wants to confront mainstream as well as unconventional ideas based on reason and coherent arguments. A double-blinded peer-review process ensures the consistency of arguments, but authors are invited to argue against criticism if they believe the reviewers' verdicts are influenced by political or ideological views.

The book series thus aims to help readers to understand divisive issues in sport better through indiscriminate presentation of arguments of clearly defined sides, including those that do not match with the predominant narrative of being "correct". Our hope is that this will stimulate readers to sharpen their own critical thinking.

Verner Møller and Jörg Krieger

ATHLETES PRESSING CHARGES

FIGHTING FOR THE FUTURE OF MODERN PENTATHLON

JÖRG KRIEGER

First published in 2022
as part of the *Sport & Society* Book Imprint
doi: 10.18848/978-1-957792-05-7/CGP (Full Book)

Common Ground Research Networks
2001 South First Street, Suite 202
University of Illinois Research Park
Champaign, IL
61820

Copyright © Jörg Krieger 2022

All rights reserved. Apart from fair dealing for the purposes of study, research, criticism or review as permitted under the applicable copyright legislation, no part of this book may be reproduced by any process without written permission from the publisher.

Library of Congress Cataloging-in-Publication Data

Author: Krieger, Jörg.
Title: Athletes Pressing Charges: Fighting for the Future of Modern Pentathlon / by Jörg Krieger
p. cm.
ISBN 978-1-957792-04-0 (pbk: alk. Paper) – ISBN 978-1-957792-03-3 (hardcover: alk. Paper) – ISBN 978-1-957792-05-7 (pdf)

Library of Congress Cataloging-in-Publication Data

Names: Krieger, Jörg, author.
Title: Athletes pressing charges : fighting for the future of modern
  pentathlon / Jörg Krieger.
Description: Champaign, IL : Common Ground Research Networks, 2022. |
  Includes bibliographical references. | Summary: "Athletes Pressing
  Charges explores the athlete-led protest movement in the Olympic sport
  of modern pentathlon. The athlete activists protest against the removal
  of the horse-riding discipline from the sport and blame the sport's
  governing body, the International Modern Pentathlon Union, for violating
  good governance principles and mismanagement"-- Provided by publisher.
Identifiers: LCCN 2022011245 (print) | LCCN 2022011246 (ebook) | ISBN
  9781957792033 (hardback) | ISBN 9781957792040 (paperback) | ISBN
  9781957792057 (pdf)
Subjects: LCSH: Union Internationale de Pentathlon Moderne. | Pentathlon. |
  Sports administration. | Protest movements.
Classification: LCC GV1060.75 .K75 2022 (print) | LCC GV1060.75 (ebook) |
  DDC 796.06/9--dc23/eng/20220506
LC record available at https://lccn.loc.gov/2022011245
LC ebook record available at https://lccn.loc.gov/2022011246

Editorial Assistant: Patricia Alonso Membrilla
Cover Image Credit: Christopher J West (Website: https://chriswestdesign.wixsite.com/)my-site

TABLE OF CONTENTS

Preface	*XIII*
Abbreviations	*XVII*
Introduction	1
The Approach	7
Modern Pentathlon	21
The Movement	33
Oppression of Athletes' Voices	59
Disregard for Principles of Governance	73
Conclusion: The Big Picture and Wider Implications	103
Afterword: Response to Reviewers	*113*
Notes	*121*

PREFACE

I must admit that I have never seen any modern pentathlon competition, outside of the Olympic Games. Some might argue that this makes me an unqualified investigator into the sport. I agree that I certainly lack the technical understanding that other experts have, especially when it comes to horse riding. This, however, is not the point of this study. In fact, I would argue the opposite way around. The fact that I have no connection, no prior involvement, and, frankly, only a small interest in the sport, puts me in a good position to study the current developments. I would therefore like to make clear that without any detailed knowledge on horse riding, I do not have a personal standpoint on the debate concerning whether equestrianism should be part of modern pentathlon or not. I do take animal welfare concerns seriously; a view shared by the community of athletes involved in modern pentathlon.

So what caught my interest in this case? During my short time in academia, I have come into contact with the histories of different governing bodies of sport. I recently explored the entire history of World Athletics. The study served to further solidify the problematic history of the modern sport movement, as it exposes corrupt organizational cultures, racism, sexism, anti-Semitism, and authoritarian sympathies within the history of the federation. When I was confronted with the issues within the International Modern Pentathlon Union, I could see the similarities between the past mismanagement of other sport organizations and the accusations made with regards to the situation in the International Modern Pentathlon Union. However, the concerns about the International

Modern Pentathlon Union's questionable policies take place in the here and now, whereas my previous studies had mainly tackled the past. The acuteness of the situation motivated me to dive into this topic.

Centering the voices of athletes, as I do throughout this study, adds an important dimension to the scientific understanding of the governance issues in modern pentathlon. Research on the marginalization of athletes in decision-making in international sport is continuously increasing and this research complements the work done by my colleagues. I will present the state of research in the main text. By focusing on athletes' opinions, the study is an attempt to make unheard voices known. In contrast to my neutrality on the horse-riding matter, I do take a different starting point regarding the athletes' voices and the issues the activists raise. Through engaging extensively with the activists, I realized that it is impossible to set aside personal values and retain complete neutrality when it comes to the disregard of athletes' voices. Rather, I reflected that my work empowers the group of athletes to expose power relations that keep them away from taking influence in decision-making processes within their sport. There is a long tradition of such a paradigmatic approach in the humanities and social sciences, including sport sociology,[1] but there are relatively few studies in which the athletes' voices on a matter of sport governance are emphasised as much as in this book.

The unique access to internal insights and the interactions of a group of activists within an Olympic sport provided an opportunity to adopt the described approach. Access to such sources is usually limited, whereas as researchers we are accustomed to hearing the views of leaders within specific sports. To my best knowledge, a movement of outspoken opposition against a governing body of sport that includes many of the very best athletes in the sport is extremely rare. Critical researchers often struggle to get access to first-hand material, including archival material that sport organizations might hold back. Therefore, my biggest acknowledgement goes to the brave athletes and other involved individuals from the modern pentathlon community, who had the courage to speak up within the framework of this research project.

In a recent publication on good governance in sport, Arnout Geerært and Frank Von Eekeren highlighted in their foreword that sport organizations are continuously praising good governance in sport. However, they argue, it would be a "fatal mistake" if academics join the chorus and turn away from investigating governance in sport. "The public discourse has changed dramatically, but the realities of sport lag behind," Geerært and Von Eekeren continue.[2] This study takes their warning seriously and continues the investigations into governance issues in sport by centering athletes' voices.

Attentive readers will note that I am based at a university in Denmark and that it is the Danish Modern Pentathlon Federation that brought the International Modern Pentathlon Union before the Court of Arbitration of Sport. Therefore it is particularly important to stress that I do not have any links to the Danish Modern Pentathlon Federation and was not involved in the lodging of the Court of Arbitration of Sport case. I further did not contribute to any preparation of the Court of Arbitration of Sport case.

Readers should bear in mind that the developments within the athletes' movement as well as within the International Modern Pentathlon Union is an ongoing process at the time of the final submission of this manuscript to the publisher in March 2022. The athlete movement only formed in November 2021, a decision on a potential replacement for horse-riding at the 2028 Los Angeles Olympic Games has not been made, and the modern pentathlon season is only about to begin in the spring. However, the focus of this study on the accusations of the activists allows for the publication of the first interim results. Further investigations should follow. It remains to be seen whether this is in the form of a defense formulated by the International Modern Pentathlon Union's leadership or an independent investigation triggered and supervised by other individuals or organizations. For now, this study focuses on the protest movement in modern pentathlon and discusses a unique, athlete-led movement that presses charges against that sport's governing body.

This academic book is published within the book series of "Sharp Ideas in Sport". The series allows authors to respond directly to academic reviewers', who have reviewed an earlier version of the text for validity and suitability for publication. We, as editors of the book series, see this feature as a possibility for authors to defend their viewpoints and to potentially reject suggestions made by the reviewers based on solid arguments. I will respond to the reviewers of my manuscript following the main text. Readers, who take issue with my "one-sided" approach, as one of the reviewers called it, are strongly recommended to read my response to such criticism at the end of this book.

Finally, I want to acknowledge my colleagues Verner Møller, Ask Vest Christiansen, Anders Schmidt Vinther, and April Henning. I also want to thank the two unknown peer-reviewers, who provided valuable comments to improve the manuscript. Michael Connolly worked on the language of the manuscript with me. Emilie Møller Ibsen supported the reseach process. Phillip Kalantzis-Cope of the Common Ground Research Networks supported my enthusiasm for this project and was willing to speed up the production of the book due to the urgency of the topic. Finally, I need to thank my wife Eunkyung and my two children Teo and Yuna, who gave up some of their time with me so I could work intensively on the book.

ABBREVIATIONS

ASOIF	Association of Summer Olympic International Federations
CAPM	Confederation of African Modern Pentathlon
CAS	Court of Arbitration of Sport
FEI	International Equestrian Federation
IF	International Federation
IOC	International Olympic Committee
MPADK	Danish Modern Pentathlon Association
NF	National Federation
NGO	Non-governmental organization
NOC	National Olympic Committee
OCR	World Obstacle Racing
SGO	Sports Governance Observer
UIPM	International Modern Pentathlon Union
UIPM AC	International Modern Pentathlon Union Athletes' Committee
USAPM	USA Pentathlon Multisport

INTRODUCTION

> *"This could be the end of the sport"*
> (Joe Choong, Olympic champion in modern pentathlon
> at the 2020 Tokyo Olympic Games)

Changes to technical aspects of a sporting discipline often provoke strong reactions such as the one quoted above by the current Olympic champion in the men's modern pentathlon, Joe Choong (Great Britain). Anxious athletes, fearing for their personal future in the sport - or indeed spectators, often concerned about the modernization of enshrined customs - voice such apocalyptic scenarios publicly when faced with new changes to rules by governing bodies of sports. For example, the introduction of the Virtual Assistant Referee in football or the possibility to challenge decisions in tennis led to similar public outrage. Discussions on the ownership of a sport follow with the public contesting an ideological debate with sport organizations. The discussions center around the question of "who owns a sport?".

Yet, the case of modern pentathlon goes far beyond mere technical changes and might indeed lead to the end of the sport as we know it. The sport's international governing body, the International Modern Pentathlon Union (UIPM), decided in November 2021 to cease the horse riding event after the 2024 Paris Olympic Games. Historically consisting of the five disciplines of running, shooting, fencing, swimming, and horse-riding, the UIPM is prepared to proceed with this significant step on the back of incidents at the 2020 Tokyo Olympic Games when several athletes encountered severe difficulties with their horses. The UIPM leadership justifies the radical step with a need to modernize the sport in an attempt to secure its place on the Olympic programme. Indeed, the International Olympic Committee (IOC) reviewed the sports programme at the Olympic Games in December 2021 and preliminarily removed modern pentathlon from the disciplines selected for the 2028 Olympic Games and beyond.[1] However, the IOC's temporary removal of modern pentathlon was a consequence of the UIPM not presenting a new fifth discipline and not having a "complete" sport at this time. It was not a reaction to the problems occurring in Tokyo.

Without doubt, the removal of the horse-riding discipline would transform the sport of modern pentathlon significantly, severely challenging those who are currently engaged in the sport on all levels. Young athletes who only spent a few years practicing the sport, current elite competitors who have dedicated their lives to the sport, and more experienced athletes close to retirement - many of whom plan to pursue a coaching career - are all massively affected by the change. Thus, it is little surprising that the planned changes caused wide-ranging protests within the modern pentathlon community. A total of 667 athletes have signed a petition handed to the UIPM, issuing a vote of no confidence in current UIPM President Klaus Schormann, demanding his resignation together with the entire UIPM Executive Board along with General Secretary Shiny Fang. In November 2021, an athlete-led group emerged in the form of Pentathlon United to organize the activities in a more coordinated and official manner. Pentathlon United opened a Twitter account to publicly voice discontent about the actions of the UIPM and provide a platform for its initiatives. Pentathlon United also approached involved stakeholders within international sport. For example, the group submitted a letter to IOC President Thomas Bach, signed by 46 Olympic medalists protesting the UIPM decision.

This study is significant because the current debates on modern pentathlon's disciplines need to be considered against the backdrop of increasingly stronger attempts by athletes from semi-professional Olympic sports to make their voices heard in decision-making processes. In recent years, athletes in many countries turned to collective action to gain a greater say within their sport. Independent athletes and player associations have been established at the national, regional and international levels that advocate for collective action and multi-stakeholder engagement.[2] This development is also a consequence of ongoing governance issues such as power abuse, corruption, money laundering, racism, sexism, and clientelism within international governing bodies of sport. Therefore, this study has broader significance for the ongoing challenges by athletes and athletes-led organizations on powerful sport organizations.

This study's point of departure is the existing power imbalance between sport organizations and athletes.[3] It is argued that by providing a voice to the group of athlete activists, who have limited power vis-a-vis the UIPM, a contribution can be made to understand the ongoing issues in modern pentathlon. Whilst those in power (the UIPM) have the means to share information, the disempowered (the group of athletes) did not previously share this possibility. Thus, a conscious decision was made to work principally with the athletes' voices to provide the marginalized athlete community with a possibility to present their views. Based on this starting point, the data collected from the activists through interviews, documentation, and observation was then the subject of a rigorous analysis and comparison with the UIPM's viewpoints presented in the public domain, in addition to internal documents such as Congress minutes in which the UIPM leadership extensively explain their views.

This study has a threefold aim. First, it analyzes the activist movement by focusing on its establishment and the activists' main motivations. Second, it attempts to detangle the complexity of the ongoing governance issues within the UIPM by exploring the activists main accusations. Third, it situates the modern pentathlon case within the broader discussion of athletes' representation in (Olympic) sport.

Taken together, this work builds upon the overall understanding of the debate and provides indications for further examinations of the case. It is argued that the group of activists is not a group of revolutionaries who are solely interested in gaining power. The group genuinely represents athletes' interests and allows athletes with a much-needed platform to voice their concerns. Moreover, the strong demands for a complete, external, and entirely transparent investigation into the UIPM leadership appear justified.

The book supersedes the structures, constitutions, and governance principles installed within the UIPM. Whilst the measurement of rules and procedures, as undertaken in recent years by the Danish Non-Governmental Organization (NGO) Play The Game, provides a valuable tool to assess the working practices of sport organizations, they do not "measure the real-life governance practices of the international federations."[4] The investigation on hand goes a step further and analyses how those opposed to the UIPM's actions perceive the reality of decision-making within the federation's structures. Or, in other words, it aims to uncover "the evidence that contradicts official wisdom."[5]

This study serves to provide context for the ongoing issues in the UIPM and to provide an initial, compact form of the allegations made. Its starting point is the assumption that athletes' voices are effectively neglected in international sport, and therefore room must be provided for athletes' views. Many athletes in other lower-revenue, non-unionized sports have recently experienced such side-lining. For example, World Athletics stripped away throwing events in its Diamond League events without consulting the athletes. Therefore, this study should be viewed as a starting point for potential further investigations and not be mistaken as an investigation that has a mandate to fully investigate the alleged claims by the protesters.[6]

CHAPTER 1

The Approach

The Broader Picture of Athletes' Voices in Sport

The question "who owns a sport?" is as old as modern sport itself. Ever since the concept of competitive sport emerged from British public schools in the nineteenth century, individuals from different nations, classes, races, and gender have debated who should be allowed to participate in sporting activities. The most prominent restriction for participation was the invention of the amateur concept that prevented lower classes from competing.

It is generally acknowledged that the international sport federations (IFs) are the organizations with full control over individual sports (or several sports as in the case of the International Skiing Federation). However, there is no global legal foundation for the monopoly enjoyed by IFs.[1] The right to govern a sport is awarded through the IOC. Rule 26, point 1.1. states that the mission of an IF within the Olympic Movement is to "to establish and enforce, in accordance with the Olympic spirit, the rules concerning the practice of their respective sports and to ensure their application."[2] The organizational pyramid in international sport sees the IFs with near-total control over sporting governance, with national federations (NFs), regional federations, and clubs subject to comply with the IFs' rules and regulations.[3]

The global sport system has been the subject of increased scrutiny in recent years, thanks to the work of investigative journalists and academics, but also due to courageous whistleblowers who came forward and reported abuses of power, corruption, and doping in sport. The bribery scandal around the 2002 Winter Olympic Games in Salt Lake City resulted in reform attempts,[4] but wrongdoings have continued to surface since then. Amongst many others, the International Federation of Association Football, World Athletics, and the International Biathlon Union have faced major corruption scandals. A major problem prevails, however, as the control of good governance principles remains within the sport system whose autonomy is strongly protected by its stakeholders.[5]

There are many involved groups, such as commercial partners, broadcasters, or clubs, that control different aspects of a sport. Athletes, however, are one key stakeholder group that has historically been kept away from decision-making and continues to find itself marginalized from debates centered around governance. In recent years, athletes have begun to make attempts to disrupt such traditionally rigid governance structures. Scholar Peter Donnelly even went as far as to argue that "players (and fans) have become the utensils of historymakers."[6] However, the number of voices amongst athletes who want to be put on a fair footing with sport administrators within the governance of sport is rising exponentially. Encouraged by the impact of recent social protest movements such as #MeToo or Black Lives Matter within the field of sport, they speak out against their perceived discrimination by referencing human rights.[7] The World Players Association, founded in 2014, predated those movements by several years and became an important pioneer.[8] In parallel to this, a sport and human rights movement is gaining momentum. One that has its origin in the human rights impact of mega-sport events and increasingly influences governance discussions in international sport, including athletes' representation.[9]

Athletes form the base of international sports' organizational pyramid.[10] Activism within the modern pentathlon community must be understood against the background of ongoing developments towards independent athletes' representation in semi-professional (Olympic) sports.[11] In Germany, athletes founded an independent organization, Athleten Deutschland, to represent the interests of athletes in 2017. A year later, athletes from around the world established Global Athlete, an institution that understands itself as a collective to tackle the power balance between athletes and administrators. The same development can be witnessed in individual sports. The Athletics Association attempts to unify athletes' voices in the sport of track-and-field, and in July 2021, the International Swimmers' Alliance was formed with the same goal for the sport of swimming. The athletes argued that the governing bodies had failed to consider the opinions of the athletes as the most integral stakeholders of sport.[12] Taken together, scholar Maximilian Seltmann argues correctly that "the progressive institutionalization of athletes depicts a new challenge to the power structures of the existing [international sport] system."[13]

Recent demands of athletes are important because historic power structures within the international sport system have held strong over time, changing slowly if at all. This holds particularly true for the Olympic Movement. "The IOC is a remarkably stable group that protects its interest to an impressive degree," argues American scholar Jules Boykoff.[14] Consequently, there are only a few allies that protest groups can rely on when challenging the main stakeholders within the so-called "Olympic family." Exposure of the marginalization of athletes is growing. For example, talking about the 2022 Winter Olympic Games in Beijing (China), the German alpine skiing director Wolfgang Maier complained in a documentary in January 2022 that athletes are being abused for commercial and political goals of the IOC. Consequently, Maier said, he had "personally no appreciation for this institution."[15]

However, athletes today have the possibility to share information transnationally which helps them to amplify their messages.[16] In particular, the newly emerging athlete-led bodies challenge the traditional form of athletes' representation through athletes' commissions/committees. The idea to integrate athletes via internal working groups stems from the early 1980s, when the IOC created an IOC Athletes' Commission to reflect athletes' desire to contribute to the future of the Olympic Movement.[17] As a rule, active athletes vote for their athletes' bodies' representatives (either active or recently retired athletes) at world championships or the Olympic Games, with some organizations reserving the right to appoint additional members.

Critics argue that the athletes' committees have consultative roles within the governing bodies of sport, but lack influence in decision-making processes.[18] Whilst an increasing number of sport organizations have awarded a seat to the athletes committee's chair in their sport, the athletes are kept away from power. The UIPM Athletes' Committee (UIPM AC) serves as a good example here. The UIPM AC is composed of seven athletes from different nationalities in an attempt to represent athletes' opinions from all continents.[19] Only athletes who have been ranked internationally within the past two seasons of voting are eligible to run for a place on the committee. The lack of influence for the athletes is best demonstrated by their lack of voting power. Whilst the Chair of the UIPM sits on the UIPM Executive Board, the individual only holds one vote. In the General Assembly, the UIPM AC is also allowed to vote together with all NFs. Critics, however, argue that such marginal influences on decision-making are only of a symbolic nature and therefore have suggested the introduction of veto rights for athletes as a means of strengthening their position.[20]

Beyond such statutory restrictions, recent critical research has revealed severe limitations to the independent work of athletes' commissions. For example, some IFs have a section included in their Code of ethics that prevents athletes from making "adverse comments."[21] In the IOC, Athletes' Commission members have to swear the Olympic oath as they are considered to be IOC members and therefore have to acknowledge that they act in the interest of the organization.[22] Ahead of the 2020 Tokyo Olympic Games, IOC Athletes' Commission member Hayley Wickenheiser received criticism from the IOC for calling for a postponement of the Games. She was told she should have spoken to the IOC first, restricting her freedom of expression. "They like to try to contain the message and have one message, but I don't think a democratically elected institution like the IOC should be censoring its members, especially in times like this," Wickenheimer claimed.[23] In another example, the IOC and its Athletes' Commission are challenged for failing to address and acknowledge criticism of the IOC Athletes' Declaration.[24] Scholars have also criticized the secretive approaches of sporting bodies' commissions within the medical-scientific field. For example, in the case of hyperandrogenism rules in sport, there has not as yet been any systematic athlete consultation.

Importantly, the public narrative and the rhetoric of the sport organizations around the issue of sport organizations tells a different story. When American athlete Fan Xiao voiced concerns about the staging of the 2020 Tokyo Olympic Games, the IOC responded by highlighting the organization's commitment to athletes' involvement in decision-making on a full page. The IOC also highlighted its "longstanding support and respect for athletes' rights."[25]

In response to the ongoing governance crisis with regards to athlete involvement, researchers have started to explore the issue of representation in-depth over the past years. Research projects on employment relations of athletes in Olympic sports,[26] strengthening the representation of athletes' sport organization's management and governance, as well as dedicated special issues in academic journals have been created to improve and evaluate the topic.[27] Researchers are mostly in agreement that despite partial success by single athlete unions and recently emerging independent athletes organizations, the conditions for athletes remain unacceptable and easily exploited by governors of sport.[28] Some scholars acknowledge that improvements have been made in the past decade, but "athlete representation and power remains a matter of ongoing contestation."[29]

It is important to contextualize the activism in modern pentathlon against the background of these important developments and continuing shortcomings within the Olympic system. Scholar Helen Lenskyj has summarized the current situation within the Olympic system fittingly: "As the Olympic industry faces resistance from within the ranks of athletes and sport administrators, as well as from community activists, media critics, and academic researchers, it cannot afford to ignore the winds of change."[30] It appears that Olympic sport is at a crossroads with modern pentathlon activists pointing out that the UIPM missed the decisive turn. Therefore it is important to provide the athletes and supporting activists with the space and platform to make their opinion known.

The Starting Point

Based on this imbalance of athletes vis-a-vis the governing bodies of sport, I adopt a critical constructivist viewpoint for the purpose of this study. In doing so, I argue that a single interpretative truth must be denied because the research process is always mediated through an individual person, the researcher. It is important to embrace subjectivity, particularly when there is close contact between the researcher and the study group.[31]

Throughout the past several decades, social scientists have had to contend with the fact that social research is an inherently intersubjective field. Rather than ignore the relationship the researcher has to the people with whom they are working, it is better to address one's position in terms of power, influence, and solidarity. This is especially the case when studying marginalized communities, whose voices are often unheard, and need to be protected, but the researcher maintains a powerful position in how they depict the lives and values of "others." Without including one's own subject position, anthropologists argued that this process actually reified a notion of an objective interpretive style of writing. For example, it has been noted that scholars must reconcile their own position in the political economy of research by reflecting on how their own subject position impacts the direction of research.[32]

I take the starting point for the purpose of this study to be the view that the playing field in international sport is not equal. This stance speaks directly to the World Players Association's pathway for the reform of global sport. Amongst the six proposals by the World Players Association's we find "put people first" and a call for "collective action" that reflects values from the political left.[33] This shift in perspective is particularly important when studying the critical process of workers trying to organize in the midst of precarious working conditions, which reflects the current situation of athletes.[34]

In doing so, this study is situated within a critical social research framework, which "sits in stark contradiction to common-sense understanding of scholarly research as a process of disinterested information gathering, based on the concept of value neutrality."[35] As mentioned, taking on the position of the critical social researcher is considered an academic exercise here. I do not take on the position of the activist myself. Rather, I follow the important distinction made by scholar Ian McDonald, who argues that "critical social research is concerned with the production of knowledge, while political activism is concerned with securing practical changes."[36] Both approaches reject value-neutrality, but whereas critical social research produces the resources for subordinate groups - such as athletes - political activists use the research in their campaigns against those in positions of authority. It is the former approach that drives the analysis in this study. Thus, this research aims for a better understanding of athletes' oppression and the governance issues within the UIPM. The study does so by working closely with the collective of people who are subject to those conditions.[37] Naturally, this does not mean that the activist group's statements can stand for themselves in this study. Rather, they are critically assessed and contextualized through a comparison with the publicly available statements and information from the UIPM leadership as well as the UIPM's direct engagement with athletes and other protesters. Moreover, the activists' accusations about the UIPM's mismanagement of the sport are guided by literature on good governance principles in sport.

Some readers might question the consistency of the approach considering the fact that the activists in modern pentathlon defend the conservation of a sport, displaying many hallmarks of conservative ideology. They argue for tradition and sustaining horse-riding. However, as we will see, they do not argue for a freeze on development. Rather, at the core of their arguments stand accusations about outdated organizational cultures and structures that, according to the activists, have hindered innovation in the sport and given rise to problems with horse-riding in the first place. Thus, a discussion that focuses merely on the decision to drop horse-riding is too unilateral. Conversely, the adopted starting point assists in widening the perspective on the current state of modern pentathlon.

Concepts and Methods

In an attempt to understand the position adopted by the activists against the current UIPM policies, this study utilizes James Jasper's framework to study social movements. Jasper explores various examples of how different social movements work and argues that "to understand what and how people organize themselves against things they dislike, we need to know what they care about, how they see their place in their world, [and] what language they use to describe entities (...)."[38] He calls for an exploration of the main individuals involved, an identification of the interactions between the protesters as well as between protesters and oppressors, and a detailed investigation into the main arguments of those promoting change. Jasper's work is useful here because he argues that political conviction is closely tied to human emotions. He writes: "A collective identity or boundary does not motivate us to act simply because we understand it; we must care about it. It *means* something to us".[39] As we will see, the athletes are deeply involved with their sport and identifying strongly with the modern pentathlon athlete community. In result, their responses to the UIPM decision were strongly driven by emotions. This finding makes Jasper's theories particularly relevant for this study.

Yet, understanding protesters and activists is only possible if one can get close to the subjects and communicate with them indepth and directly. Therefore, the main sources of information for this study were individuals who oppose the current UIPM policy. Extensive contact with the leaders of the activist group was made in an attempt to understand the meanings and decisions of the activists. This provided context and insights unavailable in the public sphere, assisting the knowledge gathering about the activists and their arguments. I engaged with the positions and arguments of the UIPM leadership via their statements from the extensive, publicly available sources including official press releases, interviews, UIPM minutes, and UIPM rules and regulations. The UIPM has the means to share information publicly and did so extensively in the period from August 2021 until February 2022. The engagement with the UIPM material also meant that some of the accusations of the interviewees were not included in this book because they appeared to be too speculative.

Initial contact was made through a gatekeeper - an individual involved in modern pentathlon - who provided access to the leaders of the activist group. The gatekeeper is not one of the leaders of the activist group. Following the first interviews, the individuals involved provided further contacts who supported the data collection process. In-depth, open interviews were conducted over a period of two months between December 2021 and February 2022; some were interviewed several times. Some interviewed individuals also contacted the researcher outside the process so that the researcher became increasingly engaged with the group over time. Such commitment to the group allowed for additional insights to learn about the developments within the group by continuously interrogating activists about their actions.[40]

Open interviews were selected as the interview technique for this study. The interviews were all between 20 minutes and 80 minutes in length and conducted in English.[41] This allowed the identification of several key topics such as engagement, motivation, anxieties, accusations, strategies, and goals to be discussed with the interviewees. The topics slightly changed depending on the involvement/role of the interviewee within the modern pentathlon community. However, rather than the researchers steering the interview, the participants navigated the topics and foregrounded the issues that appeared to be of most relevance to them. The activist leadership further allowed the researcher to observe their online meetings to receive additional insights. The researchers' involvement with the group concluded at the beginning of February 2022. Thus, the analytical focus lies on the processes behind the removal of horse-riding rather than on the debates about the new discipline that are ongoing.

The interviewed individuals included current elite athletes in the sport of modern pentathlon, former athletes (defined in this study as anyone who has competed in the sport on an international level during his/her lifetime), coaches, representatives of NFs, representatives of international athlete organizations, and other insiders of the sport. In total, 38 interviews were conducted. Most of the interviews (27) were conducted with active athletes or athletes who have retired within the last two years. The sources' viewpoints encompass various national perspectives. Individuals from 22 countries were interviewed for the study, including at least one athlete from each continent. Participants from the Global North (majority) and Global South (minority) took part in the study. No more than four individuals from one country have been included in the study to prevent national views distracting from the overall viewpoints. All interviewed current athletes compete in the sport on the international level.

Considering that modern pentathlon is an Olympic sport practiced by relatively few competitors on the elite level, the sample size and breath is comparatively high. The fact that the interviewed athletes provided contacts to additional athletes after the interviews demonstrates the solidarity within the activist group and the athletes' community in the sport. In fact, more athletes were available for interviews but a selection had to be made due to the lack of English language knowledge for some athletes.

The activists also served as informants in the study, and made available documents and minutes that could otherwise not be obtained. For example, the working books of recent UIPM congresses are not publicly available on the UIPM website. However, their contents include reports and statements by individuals from the UIPM leadership and UIPM bodies that proved to provide valuable insights for this study. The fact that such documents are not available to the general public will be addressed further below.

Throughout this research, all personal information of the interviewed individuals is removed. Within the group, there is a high degree of anxiety that their communication could be monitored. As discussed later in the book, those concerns proved to be correct when athletes identified UIPM Executive Board members entering the athletes' *WhatsApp* and *Telegram* group chats with fake names. Some fear political consequences if their identity is revealed. For example, in a letter sent by Russian athletes to the UIPM, in which they voice their opposition to the removal of riding and the Russian NFs support for the decision, an addendum read: "P.S. Due to safety of athletes and possible threats which could follow after their signatures will be written we can not write down their names. But we invite you to come to Russia, visit all regions and learn athletes' strong opinions against removal of riding."[42] On the grounds that this research focuses on the activists, it was established that confidentiality for individual human subjects in this study could be granted. As some countries have only one or very few elite competitors in the sport, it was further decided to refrain from listing the nationalities of the interviewees. However, readers should know that at least one quote of each interviewed subject has been included in the main text.

Two entities are the main focus of the study. First, "the activists" of individuals and federations who oppose the drop in horse-riding and the current policy-making of the UIPM. Jasper's definition of a group as a small, informal gathering or network is utilized here.[43] As we will see, the athlete-led group are not only reactive protesters, expressing dissent. Rather, they are proactive in their attempts to change the sport of modern pentathlon in its traditional form. Thus, while they are resisting change, they are also engaged in reform, but have a different understanding on how this reform should look like than the UIPM. It is important to note that not all individuals in the leadership of the activist group always shared the same opinion. In fact, when the athletes first discussed the initial petition to remove the UIPM President and the entire Executive Board, there were different opinions on what to demand in the letter. Importantly, when such differences occurred, the opinion of the present athletes was followed. In this study, I will refer to "the activists" when the large majority of interviewed individuals share the same viewpoints or if public information is provided.

The second entity is the "UIPM leadership," which oversees an organization (the UIPM) which has statutes, regular meetings, elected leaders, and legal status. There are other organizations named in the study, such as the IOC, National Olympic Committees (NOCs), or NFs, who generally share those characteristics with the UIPM. Just as with the activists, a differentiated and nuanced analysis is required when focusing on the UIPM leadership. For example, when a source claimed that "the UIPM" acted wrongly on an issue, this required a follow-up question on whether such criticism was targeted at specific individuals, the entire UIPM Executive Board or a distinct group of individuals. As the decision to remove horse-riding was made unanimously by the UIPM Executive Board, the criticism of this process can be targeted to all individuals on the Executive Board. In contrast, the activists argue that more strategic moves such as the acquisition of more member federations to maintain the power balance in the federation were initiated by Klaus Schormann, President of the UIPM, and a close group of individuals around him. This specific core group of leaders, who have been in power for several decades, will be defined later in this text. When the term "UIPM leadership" is used in the following, it will refer to the current group of UIPM President, UIPM Executive Board, and UIPM General Secretary Shiny Fang.

Finally, I would like to note again that I have no personal interest in the ongoing conflict between the activists and the UIPM. This research was further conducted independently and without any funding. And whilst I was in close contact with individuals who are strongly opposing the drop of horse-riding and not with the UIPM leadership, this was a conscious decision in an attempt to explore the group itself. Thus, any further action taken from this research might be guided by the findings of this study but will not be driven by the researcher personally.

CHAPTER 2

Modern Pentathlon

The UIPM is fully incorporated into the international sport system and shares core institutional features such as governance structures, financial dependencies, and legal frameworks with other stakeholders within the Olympic Movement. The UIPM is one of many IFs that govern a specific sport. According to the Olympic Charter, an IF has the right to rule over a sport autonomously, that is without direct interference from the IOC or any other rivaling bodies.

That said, modern pentathlon's history and the governance of the sport differ in various aspects significantly from other sports and IFs. It is crucial to understand those specificities as they are utilized by the different parties in the current debates. Therefore, the history and current specificities of modern pentathlon and the UIPM will be briefly outlined in the following and precede the discussion of the ongoing conflict.

A History Tied to the Olympic Games

Modern Pentathlon is a unique sport in many ways. The founder of the modern Olympic Movement, Pierre de Coubertin, laid the ideological groundwork for the sport by putting together a competition consisting of running, fencing, swimming, horse-riding, and swimming events. As a result, Coubertin is ever present in the

UIPM's marketing material of the sport until this day and is continuously mentioned in the communication around the horse-riding removal.[1] The UIPM has a Pierre de Coubertin Committee, chaired by the UIPM President and composed of experts on Coubertin. A family descendant of Coubertin is also on the Committee that deals with the promotion and memory of Coubertin's heritage.

Coubertin had presented his idea of a sport in the style of the pentathlon at the ancient Olympic Games in many writings.[2] His vision for the composition of the five sports was by no means coincidental, but reflected, according to Coubertin, the skills of "modern" soldiers, producing the complete athlete.[3] The French Baron had originally wanted to include rowing (instead of shooting) as a discipline in the modern pentathlon but had to scrap those plans for organizational reasons.[4] However, it is clear that Coubertin had a cavalry officer in mind when he compared the modern pentathlete with the modern soldiers. As such, the modern pentathlon must be considered a "sporting allegory of a military errand on horseback, on water and on land," as described by sport historian Ansgar Molzberger.[5] In addition, Coubertin aimed to speak to two different target groups with a strong focus on horse-riding. By introducing horse-riding and fencing to athletics, Coubertin wanted to spread those sports amongst the athletic community. At the same time, he wanted to encourage riders and the military to engage in athletics sports.[6]

However, without the inclusion of rowing, Coubertin's original intentions had actually never been truly fulfilled and already by the time of modern pentathlon's debut at the 1912 Stockholm Olympic Games, a compromised version had been implemented.[7] Coubertin had found enthusiastic supporters of the sport in the Swedish organizers around General Viktor Balck. Balck regarded modern pentathlon as an ideal possibility to contribute to militarization.[8] Coubertin, who wanted to open the modern pentathlon to competitors from all social classes, successfully applied for the provision of horses by the organizing committees.[9] He wrote: "I never meant to show that men who are good horsemen and trained to horsemanship can fence also and run and swim, I meant to show that runners and swimmers and fencers who, as a rule, are not of the same social standing can ride a horse and that the impossibility for them to keep a horse of their own ought not to keep them from riding occasionally. In one word, my plan was democratic (...). Those who have no horses must be provided with some."[10] This strategy remained in place until today and stands at the core of the debate around the discipline.

In the subsequent modern pentathlon competitions at the Olympic Games before the Second World War, mainly military officers participated, so the sport's military connection endured. As sport historian Sandra Heck reports, modern pentathlon "was considered not only as a play and leisure activity for soldiers, to make them forget about the cruelty of the fighting, but also as a useful preparation for possible battles in the future."[11] The advantages of the sport worked in both directions as from 1924 onwards, armies began to recruit competitors from the modern pentathlon for the military, whereas sport organizations relied on officers as the main participants within the sport.[12] With amateur regulations in place within the Olympic Movement, only upper-class cavalry officers competed at the Olympic Games. Until the early 1950s, ordinary cavalry officers were not recognized as amateurs because they were considered to ride for professional reasons (i.e. to make a living from riding).

Modern pentathlon's historical roots, linking back to both the Ancient Games and Coubertin, have strongly contributed to the sport's continuous appearance on the Olympic programme.[13] Traditionally, the IOC had valued history as an important characteristic when selecting the sports for the Olympic Games. "Heritage and tradition" appear on the list of criteria for inclusion in the Olympic Games sport programme.[14] In fact, when in 2002, modern pentathlon was on the brink of removal from the Olympic Games, the UIPM successfully built large parts of its defense on the sport's history and close links to Coubertin's heritage.[15]

That said, the IOC increasingly includes trendy sports with youthful appeal - surfing, sports climbing or skateboarding are just a few recent examples. Coupled with modern pentathlon's relatively little popularity, the sport's conservative roots makes it now vulnerable to a deletion of the programme, where it had a safe spot before. It is those difficulties to gain more attention and participation in the sport that will now be addressed.

Sporting Difficulties

Partially as a result of the sport's complex format, modern pentathlon has suffered from a lack of participation in the sport as well as limited public interest. Both issues require further elaboration to understand the complexity behind the challenges the sport faces in the modern context.

With regards to general participation in the sport, the cost of training for five separate sports - not to mention the equipment needed to train for a sport like fencing or horse-riding - limits the pool of potential athletes who are able to compete.[16] The fact that there is little prize money to be won in the sport further complicates this situation. Moreover, the public also often confuses the modern pentathlon with combined events in the sport of track-and-field, such as the heptathlon or the decathlon. Some argue that the lack of high income through sponsorships or prize money, even for top competitors, does not carry the requisite appeal for athletes. At the 2020 Olympic Games, the sport was criticized for the lack of breadth in participation as 72 athletes from only 27 nations competed at the events.[17] With such lack of universal appeal, modern pentathlon would probably not be considered a sport to be newly added to the Olympic programme in the current environment where the IOC demands worldwide participation of candidate sports.

In an attempt to increase participation and to lead competitors to participate in the "full pentathlon," the UIPM today oversees different modifications of the sport listed within the UIPM sports pyramid. These include the laser run (shooting and running), triathle (shooting, running, and swimming) and the tetrathlon (shooting, running, swimming, and fencing). The aim of engaging individuals in those sport forms is to grow global participation and provide more pathways for potential athletes to the Olympic Games.[18]

Importantly, however, the lack of participation in the sport is not a new phenomenon but has been tolerated by the IOC ever since modern pentathlon's inclusion into the Olympic programme. For example, Sweden dominated the medal table in all but one Olympic Games (1936) editions from 1912 until 1946.[19] It is further noteworthy that there is a large spread of nations competing for medals in modern pentathlon at the Olympics today. At the past three Olympic Games (2012, 2016, 2020), athletes from 14 different nations won at least one medal (of 18 available in total). In other Olympic sports, the medal distribution is much more focused on one or a few nations.[20] For example, in the winter sport of luge only eleven nations have ever won an Olympic medal, with 62% of the medals won by competitors from Germany.[21]

It is evident that the apathy towards the sport became even more transparent with the advent of television ratings as Olympic officials could now quantify the popularity of individual events. In television rankings of the Olympic Games, modern pentathlon continuously features amongst the lowest viewing figures. One of the main challenges for pentathlon was the long duration of the event. For more than 80 years, the modern pentathlon competitions at the Olympic Games were held over a period of several days, thus differing from Coubertin's original intentions to create a test for the athletes' quick-wittedness and decisiveness.[22] However, his format struggled to entice television viewers once the Olympic Games became increasingly mediatized. In response, there have been various changes to the sport to make it more appealing for television. Ahead of the 1972 Olympic Games, the originally practiced cross-country riding that best reflected Coubertin's vision of a nineteenth-century cavalry soldier, was replaced with show jumping. But the sport continued to struggle for popularity. Shortening the time of the competition to one day and combining shooting with the running portion have been the two primary efforts to make the competition easier to broadcast. Those changes, however, come at a cost for the fans in attendance. For spectators who attend the Olympic Games, watching modern pentathlon is a feat almost equal to that of the athletes. One reporter who attended the 2008 Beijing Olympic Games wrote how watching all five events meant, "you'd have to travel to three different venues and dedicate 14 hours of your day."[23] While it may have some television appeal, that may come at the cost of a limited atmosphere as fans would, understandably, likely be hesitant to devote an entire day to watching a sport that few people understand.

The latest major change in the original modern pentathlon format occurred in 2020 when the UIPM introduced a 90-minute version of the event. In this format, the equestrian will last 20 minutes, followed by 15 minutes of fencing, 10 minutes of swimming and 15 minutes for the concluding laser run. At the 2024 Paris Olympic Games, the 90-minute format will be used for the first (and maybe last) time. The 90-minutes will include horse familiarization and the riding will be staged first. Moreover, competitors will be eliminated in the different rounds with only the best twelve athletes competing in the final laser run.[24]

Selected main changes in the sport designed to increase its appeal for the media are summarized in the following table:

1996	all five pentathlon events take place in one day
1996	.22 caliber pistol event changed to 10m air pistol
2000	swimming distance changed from 300m to 200m
2009	introduction of combined event (running and shooting) as final discipline
2010	laser pistol introduced for the shooting
2013	accelerated modus in the fencing
2020	all five events held in the same stadium
2021	90-minute format introduced

Figure 1: Main changes in the sport designed to increase its appeal for the media (1996-2021)

Media researcher Stephanie Heinicke in her study on mediatization strategies of selected Olympic sports, including modern pentathlon, notes that the UIPM intended the changes to have a high impact on coverage of the sport.[25] The majority of changes came on the back of discussions with the IOC around a potential removal of the sport from the Olympic programme during which UIPM President Klaus Schormann promised a modernization of the sport.[26] However, Heinecke concludes that despite the changes, the sport remains severely restricted in its possibilities to attract the media due to the continuing length of the competition as well as low performances of the competitors compared with specialists. Therefore, it might be little surprising that a recent list of Olympic events by the American magazine *Slate* continued to list men's and women's modern pentathlon as the "next-to-worst Olympic sport," defeating only the men's 50k race walk.[27]

Major changes to the horse-riding discipline are suspiciously absent from the list of amendments made by the UIPM in recent years. The last significant change occurred for the 1972 Olympic Games when show-jumping was introduced so spectators could follow the action live on site.[28] This is despite the fact that this discipline caused negative publicity at various high-profile events over the past two decades. For example, at the 2008 Olympic Games, six riders were thrown from their horses.[29] Four years later in London, a horse fell on a competitor, whilst another athlete jumped the final obstacle underneath her horse's neck.[30]

In consequence, there have been continuous calls to the UIPM from public observers, athletes, coaches, and officials to address the problems specific to show jumping. Some of these requests were intended to protect the horses from abuse, others aimed to increase the attractiveness of the sport. Broadly summarized, the critics of the current regulations argue that the riders are not skilled enough to compete on the horses provided. Only 20 minutes are given to prepare on the horse and many horses suffer due to the rider's lack of skill. This is considered by some to represent a serious workplace safety issue.[31]

The lack of focus on horse riding issues and apparent disregard for animal welfare has led to protests from athletes before. In 2002, athletes threatened to protest against a change in horse provision at the European Championships. At the event, the UIPM wanted to trial a new rule that foresaw all three riders of relay teams to share the same horse. At the time, the UIPM President threatened the protesters that they would be banned from the world championships, but backed down when athletes refused to ride. In 2014, leading athletes reported appalling conditions for horse riding at a World Cup in Acapulco. According to some athletes interviewed for this project, the horses were of poor quality and not prepared to compete in the event. Thus, the female athletes boycotted the laser-run after the riding, and the men's event was canceled. The UIPM then controversially announced that the event was stopped due to the extreme heat, neglecting to mention the horse-riding issue.[32] The incident indicates that the UIPM was not prepared to admit the true reasons, which, according to the athletes, constituted severe animal welfare violations on the side of the UIPM and the event organizers. Crucially, it was the athletes who aimed to bring attention to the issue, not the responsible organizations.

Governance Issues

The lack of appeal and neglect of the horse-riding discipline can be partly explained via the history and current structures of the governance of the modern pentathlon. As we will see later, those protesting the UIPM's decision to remove horse-riding claim that the UIPM does not act in the interest of the sport and the athletes, but solely out of organizational interests. Therefore, it is necessary to establish a basic understanding of the UIPM's organizational structures and their historical growth.

Until after the Second World War, modern pentathlon did not have an independent governing body. Rather, the IOC controlled the sport as a result of Coubertin's heritage. There had been attempts to establish an independent modern pentathlon federation as early as 1928, following the end of Coubertin's IOC presidency (in 1925). Led by the Swede Tor Wibom, several pentathlon officials from multiple nations thought it was necessary to free the sport from the IOC in order to allow for organizational reform.[33] The attempts led to the foundation of an International Modern Pentathlon Committee under the aegis of the IOC, as the IOC did not want to lose control over the sport. Coubertin commented from retirement that an independent federation was not necessary as he opposed any rule changes from the original idea. In fact, Coubertin generally opposed IFs out of a fear that nationalistic sentiments would influence decision-making.[34] A main argument from the IOC was the fact that the infrequent competitions in the sport did not require its own governing body. On the other hand, the lack of an organization to develop the sport also meant that there was no driving force to increase participation numbers.

It was only after the Second World War that national representatives of the sport came together again during the 1948 Olympic Games to discuss a separate federation to organize events more regularly. They created an International Pentathlon Federation under the presidency of Wibom, which considered itself responsible for all competitions outside the Olympic Games. Former Swedish Olympic champions Gustaf Dyrssen and Sven Thofelt supported the foundation, with the latter acting as UIPM President from 1960 until 1988.

The IOC was prepared to move full responsibility for the sport to the new organization, but demanded that it change its name, as the individual sports including in the modern pentathlon already had their own distinct "federation." From this debate the name of the current UIPM emerged. In the following decades, the sport developed significantly and the number of NFs increased steadily due to increased international competitions. Furthermore, in 1957, the UIPM became the governing body of the winter sport biathlon (a combination of cross-country skiing and shooting), making it the only international sport federation to oversee sporting events at both the Summer and the Winter Olympic Games.

Importantly, the UIPM today continues to govern not only those competitions in which all five disciplines are organized, but also every combination of the five sports, as mentioned above. Many continental and regional competitions are contested with a reduced number of disciplines, adding to the complex nature of the sport.

The UIPM General Assembly is the organization's supreme and legislative body. It is composed of all member federations (with one vote each, if not suspended), the president; the Executive Board members (who only vote if they represent a NF) and the UIPM Athletes' Commission chair (with one vote).[35] Other, non-voting parties such as honorary presidents or invited persons may also attend the annual General Assembly meeting. In between the General Assembly meetings, the UIPM Executive Board, composed of individual members (no less than 15 and no more than 30), the presidents of the continental confederations, and chairpersons of three committees (coaches, athletes, and medical). As most other international sport federations, the UIPM has commissions (with members appointed by the UIPM Executive Board) and committees (with members elected by the General Assembly) with specific tasks. The UIPM president is a member of all commissions and committees.

The current UIPM President, Klaus Schormann from Germany, was elected into office in 1993. Schormann, a trained teacher, had previously led the German national modern pentathlon federation. Realizing the lack of interest in the sport, Schormann appears to have followed two main strategies to modernize the sport. First, he tirelessly attempted to expand the number of member federations in the UIPM. When he started as president, the UIPM had 63 members. Today, the UIPM lists 129 federations as members of the continental confederations on the official website.[36] Second, Schormann oversaw technical changes to the sport to adapt to ongoing mediatization and commercialization of the Olympic Movement (see table 1) with a significant absence of reforms to the riding discipline.

Evidently, modern pentathlon has remained on the Olympic programme throughout Schormann's entire presidency and against several threats of removal. Thus, the current UIPM President's initiatives might be considered a success. However, the organizational culture he imposed within the federation has caused critics to appear at various times - and never have they been as harsh as in the debate around the removal of horse-riding from the sport.

***

The historic uniqueness of modern pentathlon and its governance is crucial to understanding current debates within the sport. Modern pentathlon's close links to Coubertin's Olympic heritage make the sport an exception amongst all sports on the Olympic programme and particularly intriguing to see athletes opposing their federation.

Against a historical background that is characterized by adhering to tradition, dropping horse-riding from the modern pentathlon programme must be considered an extraordinary decision. Particularly in light of the UIPM publishing a press release in August 2021 stating its commitment to secure the future of riding in modern pentathlon,[37] only to officially announce the removal of riding less than three months later at the beginning of November 2021. Given those facts, the emergence of an activist movement that strongly opposed the sudden change of strategy is not surprising. Yet, the high number of protestors - those who have spoken out as well as those remaining silent for now - currently active in the sport, as well as the potency of some of the attacks on the UIPM, leave important questions to be asked. The remaining sections of this book are addressed directly to these questions.

CHAPTER 3

The Movement

The approach taken in this study is to focus on the arguments of the athletes; to contextualize their statements and to compare them with the UIPM's officially communicated viewpoints. However, before we can understand the position of the athletes and their advocates, it is necessary to understand the motivations, strategies and initiatives of the individuals involved. This allows us to assess whether the movement acts as a collective or whether the activism consists only of individual voices. This section will first look at the trigger of the activism, the UIPM's decision to get rid of the equestrian discipline, and then present the activists. The aim is to characterize the group of activists to get a better understanding of their motivations, arguments, and goals.

The Incident and Its Background

As outlined above, athletes, media, and the IOC have raised complaints about the lack of actions by the UIPM to modernize the sport - in particular the horse-riding event - throughout the past three decades. An incident at the 2020 Tokyo Olympic Games in August 2021 brought the UIPM and its leadership under fire once more and triggered the UIPM to reinforce major changes. During the riding part of the Olympic competition, the event leader Annika Schleu (Germany) had struggled to get her allocated horse Saint Boy to jump the obstacles of the course. Schleu broke down in tears as she desperately tried to get the horse to move over the obstacles, using her whip extensively. Her coach Kim Raisner touched the back of the horse several times with her fist and instructed Schleu to punch the horse "properly." Several athletes interviewed for this study were of the opinion that Schleu and Raisner had overstepped a boundary with their actions, but blamed the extraordinary situation for their actions. Raisner was eventually disqualified according to UIPM rules, whereas Schleu finished the competition far behind the medal places.[1] Schleu was not the only athlete who struggled in the riding discipline at the Tokyo Olympic Games. In total, six athletes scored zero points during the event because of problems with their assigned horse.

The available public statements produced by the UIPM leadership reveal different phases of approaches to the incident. At first, and in line with a general policy to protect the federation from criticism, UIPM President Schormann was quick out of the blocks to criticize the athletes for the incidents. He argued that the horses were of excellent quality and the riders could only blame themselves for poor performances.[2] Such a reaction to protect a governing body of sport's image has been noticed previously in research.[3] That said, many interviewed athletes highlighted that the horses in Tokyo were of high caliber. "The best horses we ever had," one athlete said. The incident in Tokyo unfolded in front of a global television audience and caused public outrage. Without question, the media images of the incident were appalling and it was obvious that the sport had to change. Social media users insulted Schleu and Raisner with tweets such as "imagine what she does to the horse when no one's watching" amongst the milder verdicts.[4] Animal rights organizations commented on the case, demanding actions against the two Germans, changes to the UIPM rules, and, for some, dropping horse-riding from the Olympic Games altogether. The German Animal Welfare Association reported Schleu and coach Raisner to the police.[5] In January 2022, the case was dropped after Schleu and Raisner agreed to pay an unknown sum to a charitable organization.[6]

In response to the increasing public pressure, Schormann publicly appeared to change the UIPM's strategy. In a September 25, 2021, guest blog on Olympic news website *Inside the Games* Schormann wrote, "[the] UIPM remains fully committed to riding as an integral part of the modern pentathlon based on the vision of Baron Pierre de Coubertin and we look forward to doing so in an ever safer, more secure way."[7] Tying his argument to the historical roots of the sport, he acknowledged that procedures had to be improved and backed slightly down from the sole blame for the athletes. Furthermore, he highlighted the centrality of horse-riding in the sport. Schormann stated that measures to improve horse welfare in the sport would be introduced with immediate effect, as already communicated by the UIPM in a press release in August 2021.[8] Therein, the need to retain the rule of unfamiliar horses and a short preparation was highlighted. The UIPM insisted that "the unpredictability of athletes riding on unfamiliar drawn horses, with only 20 minutes to establish an understanding, is part of the dramatic spectacle that makes Modern Pentathlon unique and compelling."[9] Considerations to remove horse-riding were largely absent at the time.

Interestingly, Schormann instead emphasized in much detail the positive developments in the sport. For example, he met with the President of the International Equestrian Federation (FEI), Ingmar De Vos, to discuss how the FEI could act as a consulting institution to improve the technical aspects of horse-riding and horse welfare within modern pentathlon.[10] Schormann stated in an UIPM press release his optimism to work towards an improvement of the disciplines: "I am delighted that we have the support of the

FEI along with our own expertise within Modern Pentathlon as we work towards solutions that result in improved horse welfare and athlete safety in our sport."[11] Further, the UIPM set up an internal ten-person working group to address the riding event at the 2020 Tokyo Olympic Games. At the end of September 2021, this group presented, according to the UIPM, "extensive recommendations linked to horse welfare; education of pentathletes, coaches and judges; improvements on competition routines; and changes to the competition rules."[12] In the same time period, Schormann also spoke at the general assembly of the German modern pentathlon federation at which a motion to remove horse-riding was discussed. According to one source in attendance, Schormann told the participants that such a motion would be unsuccessful in the UIPM General Assembly. Notwithstanding, the German modern pentathlon federation submitted a motion to be considered at the UIPM Congress to remove the riding discipline and for the UIPM to form a committee to decide a replacement discipline on 27 September 2021.[13]

The submission of the motion was the first time that the complete removal of riding appeared on the desks of the UIPM leadership if public records are to be believed. However, in stark contrast to his earlier blog post and his previous public defense of horse-riding, Schormann told the German news magazine *Der Spiegel* in December 2021: "Even if Annika Schleu had become Olympic Champion in Tokyo and this regrettable incident would not have happened, the step (to remove horse-riding) could not have been stopped."[14] Other UIPM leaders echoed such statements and stepped in to defend the apparent change of mind. UIPM Vice-President Joël Bouzou in an interview with the French website *20min.fr* claimed that the UIPM had indeed discussed the removal of horse-riding since 2016.[15] The two statements are in complete opposition to Schormann's earlier statements that horse-riding would definitely remain a discipline in the sport.

The decision to propose modern pentathlon without horse-riding for the Los Angeles Games was triggered - according to an UIPM press release - because of a recommendation of the UIPM Innovation Commission. This commission had been installed in 2016 review the modern pentathlon format in the context of Olympic Agenda 2020 and Olympic Agenda 2020+5. As minutes of the UIPM IC are not publicly available, it is not known whether the body previously recommended a removal of horse-riding. However, as Bouzou is a member of the UIPM IC and argued that such a move had been discussed since 2016, it is likely a debate on the issue had taken place.

On the basis of discussions between selected UIPM Executive Board members and the UIPM IC in Monaco between 28 and 30 October 2021, Schormann, according to one interviewee, called an "urgent" meeting of the Executive Board for 31 October 2021 with a few hours' notice. This was presented to the UIPM in a presentation by the UIPM leadership in November 2021. No subject for the Executive Board meeting was provided, and no minutes written. Under these hectic and special circumstances, the Executive Board decided unanimously via video call for the replacement of the horse-riding discipline for the 2028 Los Angeles Olympic Games. There was no prior consultation engaging the wider modern pentathlon community. In order to make this decision, the UIPM leadership triggered the force majeure clause in the UIPM statutes that allows the Board to circumvent a congressional decision. The UIPM Executive Board argued it was forced to act and trigger the force majeure clause due to an IOC deadline. This demanded the submission of all sports' programmes for the 2028 Los Angeles Olympic Games with the 2021 UIPM Congress taking place after that deadline.

The UIPM Executive Board did not stop here, but also recommended a thirteen points list of criteria that the new discipline should fulfill:

- Follow the Coubertin narrative of the most complete athlete
- Not fall under the governance of another IOC-recognized International Federation
- Allow for global accessibility and universality
- Be attractive and relevant for global youth and future generations
- Provide for gender equality and fairness
- Meet sustainability and legacy requirements of IOC Olympic Agenda 2020+5
- Be exciting and easily understandable for TV / digital audiences and all sports fans
- Be low-cost for both athletes and organizers (lower equipment costs and fewer officials)
- Result in minimal injury rates and be easy to learn and train based on athletes' existing skills
- Not cause transportation and logistical complications
- Fit inside new Pentathlon Stadium and urban settings
- Be compatible with new 90-minute elimination format
- Be compatible with current handicap start and continuous event concept

It is evident from the list that the UIPM aims to address the popularity and organizational issues with the proposed changes. Media and marketing appeal dominate the criteria.

Following the official announcement of the decision at the beginning of November 2021, varying, but interlinked, reasons for the necessity of the change were given to different target groups. The Confederation of African Modern Pentathlon (CAPM) was informed that the removal of horse-riding was aimed at increasing participation opportunities.[16] In a call to pentathlon athletes, the UIPM leadership stated that the main reason was pressure from the IOC. And publicly, the UIPM argued that the change was needed to prevent the drop of the sport from the Olympic Games programme. For example, UIPM Vice-President and IOC member Samaranch Jr. stated: "We would be making a mistake if we were to take our place in the Olympic programme for granted past Paris 2024. It is not granted for us, it is not granted for anybody."[17]

Yet, before the IOC sprang into action, the UIPM Congress took place at the end of November. Whilst the UIPM Executive Board came together for the event in Monaco, all other Congress participants were only allowed to participate virtually. Originally, the motion by the German NF to remove riding had been included in the Congress agenda, even though the approval of five NFs was needed for such a motion to be accepted. However, with the Danish Modern Pentathlon Federation (MPADK) raising a court case at the Court of Arbitration of Sport (CAS) (see more below in this chapter) on the Executive Board's trigger of the force majeure clause, the UIPM leadership was warned that legal issues might arise from such a vote. Thus, the German motion was removed and a new motion included asking for permission for the UIPM Executive Board to submit a proposal to the IOC's programme commission without riding. This motion received the necessary two-thirds majority, with 66 yes votes received to 15 no votes (92 votes were possible, 81 votes casted, and three abstentions recorded).[18] Therefore, horse-riding was effectively removed from the sport after the 2024 Paris Olympic Games.

With the decision to remove horse-riding formalized but no replacement in place yet, the IOC decided to leave off modern pentathlon (together with boxing and weightlifting) from the initial programme of the 2028 Los Angeles Olympic Games.[19] The decision is provisional, with the UIPM provided with the possibility of inclusion at the 2023 IOC Session once a new fifth discipline is found. IOC President Thomas Bach highlighted that the UIPM had to demonstrate cost reduction and increase in safety, accessibility, universality and youth appeal in any future proposal.[20] Furthermore, IOC Sports Director Kit McConnell emphasized that the athletes had to play a central role in the decision-making process for the new discipline. The IOC did not comment on the drop of riding in public.

A few weeks later, the UIPM announced the formation of a "5th Discipline Working Group" to steer the identification process for a new discipline. The group includes UIPM AC members and former athletes, as well as external consultants from the media and marketing fields. The group met for the first time in January 2022 for what was described in an UIPM press release as "hugely" constructive meetings.[21]

Emergence of Activism

In light of the described general neglect of athletes' voices in international sport, one might have been surprised to see the emergence of severe protests following the UIPM Executive Boards' decision to drop horse-riding. Historically, it is not a routine occurrence for IFs to consult athletes before significant decisions are made. However, the athletes in modern pentathlon were quick out of the blocks to voice their anger about the UIPM, possibly motivated by their peers' resistance to IF leadership in other sports.

Undoubtedly, many of the individuals' engagement in the activism are driven by strong emotions against dropping the discipline of horse-riding. This is unsurprising considering the vast research undertaken on emotions as drivers of social movements.[22] "Shock," "horror," and "sadness" were just some of the reported reactions to receiving the news about the decision. "Personal" and "emotional" reasons were cited as arguments for becoming involved in the projects. One experienced athlete stated he had "sacrificed more than thirty years of my whole life" to the sport, only to be confronted with unwanted changes. However, it is necessary to explore the foundation, network, processes, and objectives of the activists further to demonstrate how their resistance is not only driven by emotional reactions but by solid arguments.

Many involved individuals stated that they had voiced concerns about the UIPM's handling of riding prior to the 2020 Tokyo Olympic Games incident. In fact, various interviewees reported that the trigger for their concerns of the UIPM's leadership was the change to the 90-minute format in 2020. Athletes had posted such discontent on their social media platforms at that time. Some interviewed athletes reported that their opinions were not taken seriously during the design process of the new format. "We had a meeting and we had our opinions, even in the UIPM headquarters (...), but we were only shown the benefit of the new format and told that it must be implemented through congress," an athlete recalled. And while athletes could provide feedback after participation in test events, they felt overlooked because they were presented with a fait accompli. One athlete even claimed that he had been informed about potential changes by insiders already in the weeks leading up to the Executive Board meeting. "But I had not anticipated that the changes would involve the removal of horse-riding," this athlete stated. One source argued: "Adaptations to the sport had been made before, but this was the first time that the fundamentals of the sport had been changed." As will be discussed below, the activists mainly suggested that the IOC leadership lacked a vision to thoroughly reform the horse-riding discipline and they made various proposals on how such a reform could manifest.

Consequently, the athletes already knew amongst themselves who was outspoken against the UIPM leadership and found it easier to create a network of activists. Eventually, very shortly after the official UIPM Executive Board announcement at the start of November 2021, the athletes created a *WhatsApp* group from which the communication and actions could be coordinated. "Within less than a day, we had hundreds of athletes in the WhatsApp group," one athlete reported. Such swift action and solidarity within the athlete community reflects the developments in other sports, for example in the creation of the Athletics Association in track-and-field.[23]

Many of the athletes had not been officially informed about the changes by that time and many found out via social media of other athletes. "It angered me that I had to get to know from other athletes," one source said. Clearly the outrage and disappointment about the decision brought the athletes of the sport together, brainstorming on how to react. The interviewed athletes remembered that there was a lot of passion and a lot of energy in the group. After a few days, non-athletes such as NF representatives and retired competitors who opposed the UIPM decision were invited to join the group, too. Importantly, there was always an understanding amongst those individuals not currently competing in the sport, that the active athletes had to lead the potential protests. For example, one retired source said that he texted an athlete to find out whether they had known about the changes in the sport: "I asked, did you know about this? She said, no I did not. This was when I started to do more research and became more active in the protests."

The activist group quickly started to coordinate joint efforts to make their discontent with the UIPM's leadership public. On November 4, 2021, the day of the official announcement to drop horse-riding, a letter signed by 667 past and present athletes of the sport was handed to the UIPM, issuing a vote of no confidence in the current leadership.[24] According to the activists, Schormann reacted by stating he did not know many of the athletes on the list. For example, current Olympic champion Joe Choong tweeted: "Anyone reading this, our President claims he only recognizes 10-15 names on a list of athletes that signed a letter against him. Just goes to show how little the UIPM care about all the athletes, or how well they actually know the sport #savepentathlon."[25] The hashtag #savepentathlon, first shared by Choong, was for many interviewed athletes outside the core pentathlon countries, the first way to engage with the activism.[26]

Similar initiatives took place in individual countries. In the United States, athletes sent a petition to the national modern pentathlon federation, demanding that the federation votes against the rule change in the UIPM Congress. Other initiatives, such as the creation of a Pentathlon United *Twitter* account quickly followed. In the following weeks, Pentathlon United became the official name for the activists under which the athletes' organized themselves. For example, Pentathlon United organized the creation of a letter of all living British and Hungarian Olympic modern pentathlon medalists together with Olympic medalists from eleven other countries addressed to IOC President Thomas Bach. The letter asked the IOC president to "save pentathlon."[27] In response, the IOC set up a meeting with the UIPM AC and a Pentathlon United representative in mid-December 2021.

Many of the interviewed athletes reported on awareness of the activist group coordinating the athletes' efforts and taking the lead. Athletes had been little informed about the processes by their federations. This was particularly the case in non-English and non-European contexts. For example, a South American athlete reported that when he reached out to fellow competitors on the continent, "they thanked me for telling me. They all supported riding, all. But they did not know anything about what was going on and did not know what to do." This exhibits a strong, collective identity within the athlete community that should not be ignored by those in charge.

Finally, the activists' attempt to make their voices known also include initiatives on the national level. In several countries, athletes organized surveys and petitions against the UIPM decision to remove riding. Those collective views were sent to the NFs in an attempt to initiate further debates on the international level.

The Horse-Riding Issue

Current and former athletes highlight that the core of the problem with the riding discipline was the devaluation of riding as a performance. It is difficult for a good rider to profit from years of experience and skills. In a "Category A" (highest level) competition, riding is not included until the final. Therefore, a pentathlete can qualify for a final without having to ride in the qualification round(s). This has left room for athletes to focus on the other disciplines and led to finalists with very poor riding skills seen in top-level competitions.

"In order to compensate for the lack of riding skills, the UIPM made the riding challenges easier and the audience became less interested in the riding," one interviewee stated. Moreover, with athletes lacking the fundamental skills to ride the horses skillfully, the high-standard animals would react in response to not consistent rider instruction, which to the observer looks rebellious and in some cases made concerns of animal welfare relevant. This is particularly a problem at the Olympic Games, one interviewee claimed: "The horse is a better quality, tracks are full up, and the riders are not used to riding that standard of horse." The horses at the Olympics horses are indeed of high standard. Consequently they are very sensible and react for example to even small displacements of the riders weight in the saddle. Inexperienced riders cannot deliver the needed accurate influence on the horse. When jumps are 120cm high, the riders need to help the horses to jump off at the right distance and less skilled rider are often not capable to achieve this. At the 2020 Olympic Games, Schleu's horse Saint Boy had already been ridden by another rider and came too close to the obstacles before jumping several times. However, Schleu was the leading athlete going into the riding discipline at the 2020 Tokyo Olympic Games. As a result, one athlete said, "there was much more media interest."

Significantly, the arguments of the activists mirror the opinion of Pierre de Coubertin on horse riding. In his "Olympic Letter XVI," originally published in 1919, he responded to criticism about the lack of possibility for individuals to participate in horse-riding, stating that methods and procedures need to be found to popularize horse-riding as sport. "Let's go work on them," Coubertin concludes.[28] According to the individuals from the activists, the UIPM - whilst not the specialized federation for equestrian sport - failed to address Coubertin's call. "Nothing has been done for riding and it has been made less important over time," one activist argued.

One frequently cited example was then 13-year old Japanese athlete Natsu Ohta, who had won the qualification event of the UIPM World Cup in Budapest in March 2021. The qualifier was contested without the riding event, and Ohta had very little experience in horse-riding and according to the UIPM website not even a riding permit.[29] When it came to the riding discipline in the final, Ohta fell from the horse, eventually finishing in 33rd place.[30] The fact that such a young competitor was put onto an experienced jump horse was heavily criticized by the activists.

"Allowing a child onto that horse, we have a duty of care (...), that was the turning point to me." Indeed, according to UIPM rules, Ohta should not have been allowed to ride during the competition, which shows a high level of irresponsibility and exposes a severe safeguarding issue by the UIPM, the NF, and the responsible coaches. One athlete argued that this episode mirrored the lack of focus by the NFs on riding just as much as the disinterestedness from the UIPM. "Many federations hand out riding licenses without seeing the athletes riding," this competitor explained and continued: "I did not have to ride to get my license, for example." Such actions can be explained with many NFs struggling to find participants in the sport.

However, instead of addressing the issues with the horse-riding discipline specifically, the UIPM decided to scrap horse-riding altogether. "My immediate reaction was 'This is an extreme response'," one athlete recalled. Some activists acknowledged that there had been many discussions on how to improve the horse-riding part of pentathlon, mainly to address horse welfare and media attractiveness, but, as one former athlete noted, "never has there been talk about a complete drop."

The activist group argues that instead of dropping horse-riding completely from the sport, there are numerous possibilities to improve the discipline. They argue that the horse welfare and athlete safety issues can be addressed if one commits to them, which leaves a change to the riding rules as the major change to be made. Regarding the latter, the group claims that the competitive value of horse-riding needs to be improved so that the athletes spend more time on the horses in training. At the same time, the overall test at the Olympic Games (i.e. the heights of the jumping obstacles) should be reduced so that more horses can be accessed to train on. At some World Cup events, such changes have already been implemented.

The group of activists does not reduce itself to merely *fight* the ongoing governance issues, however. Some individuals are actively involved in improving the quality and safety of the horse riding discipline in their countries. After all, horse-riding will officially continue to be a part of the sport until the 2024 Paris Olympic Games. Thus, whereas the UIPM seems to focus on the replacement discussions only, the activists address the problems that triggered the public outrage about the sport. "I'm all about solutions," one source said and continued: "in contrast, the UIPM only saw failure in the discipline and used the Tokyo 2020 incidents as an opportunity to get rid of it."

The athletes further provided numerous specific options on how to improve the quality and animal welfare in the horse-riding discipline. Given the athletes' experience with the sport, they were irritated that the UIPM had never reached out to them about the problems in riding. By the end of January 2022, the group intensified efforts to stage its own competitions, including horse-riding, in order to demonstrate how the discipline could work to a broader public. Therefore the group reached out to an individual with experience in organizing large-scale modern pentathlon events, with this person becoming a core member of the group. Pentathlon United's attempts to organize independent competitions mirror the strategy by individuals to create the International Swimming League that was established in 2019 to rival the competitions organized by the International Swimming Federation.[31]

Instead of solving the horse-riding issue, the UIPM leadership seems to have only pointed to the problems of the discipline, however. A telling example is UIPM Executive Board member Ivar Sisinega presenting at a press conference the poor riding performances at the PanAmerican Games. Yet, as one activist wrote via email: "it is them [the individuals on the UIPM Executive Board], who are responsible for the riding. (...) How can they sit back and

KNOW that the riding at the Olympics will be problematic and at the same time have 100% control over the rules for qualification etc." Such behavior and lack of action from the UIPM leadership indicates that there was little willingness to save horse-riding. "This is something that the UIPM wanted to do for a long time," one athlete concluded. Another athlete reported that a NF had submitted a concept to the UIPM on how the riding discipline could be reformed. Athletes were consulted for this proposed reform concept. However, the UIPM did not answer to the NF, the athlete claimed.

It is also important to note that some athletes reflected not only about the UIPM's role in the devaluation of horse-riding but also the NFs. "Every NF needs to bring its own position towards riding in the past years into question. Very few nations focused on riding and this also contributed to the lack of quality riders," one athlete explained.

Conclusively, the athletes in the activist group cited the decision to drop horse-riding as their main reason to become involved in open and secret protests against the UIPM. Many of the still-active athletes feared for their own careers and those of their colleagues in the sport. As many of the recently retired athletes continue to be active in the sport, mainly as youth coaches, they also stated concerns for the future generations they coached. Importantly, while the focus is rightly on currently active athletes, retired athletes also showed concerns about the decision. Athletes also highlighted the consequences for youth athletes, who are equally not in a position to learn a new discipline. "To compete on the top level, they must have already spent five to ten years in the sport, with riding, when they are eighteen," one athlete explained. Thus, it is certainly not only those currently competing on the highest level of the sport that are affected by the decision. On the contrary, anyone engaged in the sport will feel the consequences of the drop of horse-riding. Taken together, the activist group is of the opinion that those consequences will be solely negative for the sport.

Beyond Riding

Whilst the removal of the equestrian discipline was the main trigger for the activist group to form and motivated many individuals to engage with the movement, the majority identified bad governance and mismanagement within the UIPM as prime motivating factors. Statements communicating that governance issues stand at the core of grievances were recorded across the majority of the interviews. "As an international governing body you must make sure that the federations and the athletes are capable of taking care of the horses. They did not do that," another athlete highlighted. There was consensus amongst the active athletes in particular that the UIPM leadership had to be replaced first, then a new debate on horse-riding should be initiated.

Similarly, those few individuals involved in the leadership of NFs were primarily motivated by the alleged problems in the procedures and overall governance issues within the UIPM. The interviewed representatives from NFs appeared to be taken completely by surprise by the swift action of the UIPM Executive Board. "We were completely shocked when we heard the first rumors and those proved to be correct," recalled an NF representative.

The NFs who openly protest against the UIPM leadership argue that they act on behalf of the athletes and the modern pentathlon community in their countries. "Our sport movement is organized bottom up," one NF representative explained. Another interviewee stated that it was necessary for the NFs to become involved in the activism because of the lack of possibilities for athletes to do so. "If we do not stand up, no one will," this person claimed.

Important for the activists was that the MPADK legally challenged the UIPM Executive Board. It brought a case before the Court of Arbitration of Sport (CAS) in which it argued that the UIPM Executive Board failed to demonstrate that the situation leading to drop horse-riding was a force majeure due to the IOC's deadline for the proposal of the 2028 Los Angeles Olympic Games. The MPADK argued that there was no debate on a potential removal of riding and that the discipline was removed in "one blow," violating the UIPM constitution. The MPADK considers horse-riding to be an integral part of modern pentathlon and for the discipline to be changed, the UIPM statutes had to be changed.[32] "It was important to us (the athletes) that we saw also NFs coming forward to support the resistance. This gave especially those athletes who were anxious about speaking out in public the courage to do so," an athlete highlighted.

The MPADK further claims that the removal of riding was not the first instance in which the UIPM Executive Board enforced the force majeure clause to circumvent open congress debates. The introduction of the 90-minute format in 2020 followed the same pattern and, according to the MPADK, increased the pressure on the riding discipline. At that time, a congress could not be held due to the Covid-19 pandemic. The MPADK protested at the time and presented major concerns in a letter to the UIPM President in October 2020 regarding horse welfare. However, the concerns were waved aside with a response that the decision was final. Importantly, the athletes also identified the same pattern in the UIPM's decision-making, comparing the horse-riding removal to the change to the 90-minutes format. One athlete stated: "They called a meeting with athletes but they only showed us the benefit of the new implementation. There was no discussion, it was a decision made."

Significantly, the MPADK's case was heard first by the UIPM's

Court of Arbitration in early 2022. The UIPM statutes outline that controversies between the UIPM and member federations can be heard by the UIPM's Court of Arbitration. The MPADK argued that the UIPM should cooperate and accept direct handling through CAS as it would appeal a negative outcome in any case. The UIPM rejected this suggestion and as the MPADK does not want to risk a direct rejection through the CAS, it eventually accepted the UIPM rule requirement to first go through the UIPM Court of Arbitration. The UIPM's sole arbitrator dismissed all claims in early February 2022.

The MPADK were not alone in decrying a violation of UIPM statutes through the force majeure clause. Other interviewed individuals reported similar reactions to the announcement. "Changes to the sport always seemed to be a knee jerk reaction," one source said. "What upset me the most is the purported use of the force majeure (...) That then made me look more closely," the person continued. Thus, whilst the MPADK filed the application for a hearing at the CAS, it is evident that many athletes and other activists backed the appeal. The MPADK justified the drastic nature of the measure because it had seen with the change to the 90-minute format that the UIPM leadership did not seriously consider criticism.

Significantly, current and retired athletes do support the MPADK and try to convince other NFs to publicly speak out against the UIPM leadership. For example, in January 2022, it has been requested of Modern Pentathlon Australia to pass a vote of no confidence in the current UIPM Executive and publicly stand alongside the MPADK in its legal action. The activists have also contacted other NFs to form an international coalition of federations demanding a change in the UIPM leadership.

All athletes mentioned the governance issues and many were informed in detail about the problems they saw in the UIPM leadership. This speaks towards the athletes community's engagement with and protesting of the political processes at play in the sport. Therefore, it is important to state that NFs do not lead the way in pointing out the governance issues within the UIPM. Rather, this process is led by the athletes themselves. In fact, as will be demonstrated in the next section, the interests of athletes are given primacy within the movement.

The Main Objective

The interests of competing athletes are at the heart of the activist groups' strategies and goals. The core group, consisting during the major investigation period between three and seven individuals, is composed of past and present modern pentathlon competitors. At least one active athlete is always present at all major meetings of the group. The athletes themselves also organized meetings without any involvement of group leaders who are currently not competing. The athletes' meetings brought together groups of 20-25 individuals from different countries, who then communicated with their national athletes' communities. In reverse, the athletes communicated with the leadership of the activists via the athletes who were present in both forums. In this way, a constant exchange between the competing athletes and the activists was ensured. The leadership formed its strategic decisions based on the athletes' opinions.

Many athletes highlighted that the movement benefited immensely from the lead of Olympians, medal winners, and particularly the role of current Olympic champion Joe Choong. "Due to his recent success, he has much more possibilities to speak with individuals and receive the necessary respect from the media," one athlete said. Another interviewee added that Choong's outspokenness about the issue made the movement possible, and he was able to unite the athletes in their approach to the difficult subject matter. "In a sense," one athlete summarized, "Joe Choong is everything that Coubertin wanted to see in an athlete: a respected, outspoken role model who deeply cares for his sporting community."

Despite highlighting the significance of individual leaders of the protests, three athletes also warned that activists should be wary not to put too much responsibility into Pentathlon United. One athlete explained that the athletes "feel that there is a route to get what they want without doing too much" via Pentathlon United. Therefore, this athlete issued a warning that it was necessary that their fellow competitors continued to engage with the protests. Another athlete said: "we need to tell them that they (the athletes) are still leading it." Such concerns indicate that some athletes might be more content to take a backseat in the movement, whereas others do feel the need to drive the process.

In order to keep the athletes informed and provide them with a possibility to engage with the movement, the activist group leaders intensified efforts to establish a website for Pentathlon United from mid-January 2022 onwards. With a permanent online presence, the group wants to demonstrate that they are not a temporary group but seriously aim to challenge the UIPM leadership and improve the sport of modern pentathlon. The intensification of the efforts at the time was also a response to athletes returning to training after the winter break and in consequence having less focus on engaging with the leadership group. Thus, the website was intended to serve as a communication and exchange platform between the athletes and the Pentathlon United leadership. It went live in early February 2022.[33]

A good example of athletes taking the lead were the protests planned for the first international competitions after the winter break in 2021/22. Some athletes suggested during an athletes meeting that armbands, swimming caps, or badges could be worn that protested against the UIPM and the horse-riding removal. This suggestion was brought into the leadership group that subsequently discussed how to best support the athletes in this form of protest. Another option to voice discontent often brought up in the interviews was the possibility of boycotting future UIPM events. Many athletes saw a boycott as the only option to get the UIPM leadership to listen. However, some athletes doubted whether they would participate in a boycott of World Cup events, especially those under pressure from their NFs and those with concrete retirement plans after the 2024 Paris Olympic Games. Therefore, the activist group leaders acted much more carefully, wary of not putting the athletes at risk of direct and indirect punishments.

Importantly, by mid-January 2022 different opinions on how to proceed surfaced in the activist group's leadership. The discussions specifically focused on whether the entire UIPM Executive Board should be subject to criticism or selected individuals excepted from the critique. Those individuals within the group close to the athletes, including active athletes participating in the meetings, felt that such maneuvering was motivated by personal interests of those proposing to "pardon" individual Executive Board members. Indeed, it was surprising to see that Board members should be exempted, considering that in principle every Board member would have had the opportunity to dissent. The athletes argued against such a maneuver. One said that it was not in the interest of the athlete community because then all Executive Board members had to be considered separately. An interviewed coach confirmed that it was crucial that the athletes took the strategic lead, despite their potential lack of time. He argued: "when it comes from the athletes, there is more pressure towards the leadership." Equally significant is it to note that some athletes from federations at the forefront of the protests against the UIPM reported disagreement with their federation's self-centered approach to the issue.

Finally, the activists and the individual athletes are also aware that their attempts to challenge the UIPM leadership are restricted by a lack of financial means. "We will not win a court case against the money of the people on the other side. Money should not play the key role here," one individual stated in an email to a fellow activist. For this reason, a crowdfunding page was initiated to collect money for the activists' initiatives. Until the end of January 2022 more than two hundred individuals donated to the fundraising, accumulating around 15,000 GBP by the time of submission of this research.[34]

Costs are also a challenge for the MPADK in its legal challenge. A recent study revealed major problems with the CAS, including high costs for the CAS proceedings.[35] The cost factor adds to other threats to CAS's independence such as the court's close ties with sport organizations and conflict of interests.[36] Complaints about financial issues are usually waved aside with reference to the CAS' legal aid system. However, only 39% of the applications are granted full support, with the study questioning the low acceptance rate. For the MPADK, a comparatively small NF, the financial challenge is immense and might bring the legal case to a halt. This would lead to the movement losing an important avenue to overturn the UIPM decision. In the broader context, the situation is therefore another example of how sport's legal system is "an extension of the sports federations, where proceedings drag on irregularly and [athletes] are disadvantaged."[37]

★★★

The interviews revealed that dissatisfaction with the UIPM leadership has existed within the athlete community for a long time, and is strongly linked to issues surrounding the horse-riding discipline. The activists argue that the leadership failed to address the problems with riding despite many opportunities for reform. Thus, it is little surprising that what finally spurred the formation of the activism was the UIPM's reaction to a horse-riding scandal. In other words, the UIPM decision to remove riding has provided the motivation for modern pentathlon's athlete community to embrace a fight against the sport's leaders.

In the conversations with the activists a clear divide between exploiters (UIPM leadership) and the exploited (athletes) is revealed along socialist lines. The activists aim to overcome this divide and argue for a system of open and honest cooperation rather than cutthroat politics. A genuine belief into opportunities for athletes to directly engage in collective decision-making along the lines of participatory democracy is existent.[38] The flaws the activists see with regards to current athletes' representation will be discussed in detail later in the book.

There are smaller deviations in the strategies, mainly visible by the attempts to protect some UIPM Executive Board members from criticism. This identified tendency to leave many decisions in the hands of retired competitors might cause a watering down of the movement's convictions. Indeed, if decisions are made for other reasons than claimed commitment to athletes' representation, the activists make themselves guilty of acting dishonestly.

That said, overall the activists share a common understanding about the leading values of the movement. It is evident that all activists aim for a much more egalitarian system, rights to be heard, and advance the ideal that the athletes must be granted genuine opportunities to participate directly in collective decision-making, along the lines of a participatory democracy.[39]

It appears that the movement's main challenge is to align their progressive ideas about the governance of modern pentathlon with their conservative standpoint to retain the traditional nature of the sport. However, the activists appear to be highly aware of this discrepancy and do bring reform plans for the horse-riding discipline to the table. In fact, they argue that not the riding per se is the cause for the problems, but rather the UIPM's lack of concern for it. The group's proposals range from organizational changes over amendments to the rulebook to development strategies of riding world-wide. Some are working on concrete initiatives to demonstrate how a reformed riding competition could work and also speak to the accessibility issues within the sport. In short, they believe that a new leadership team can restore horse-riding in an attempt to keep modern pentathlon authentic to its origins whilst developing the sport into an accessible, animal-safe, and youth-appealing discipline.

Taken together, the athletes, together with sympathizers from the NFs and former athletes, have developed into a pressure group that attempts to overturn the current leadership within modern pentathlon. Their strategies and motivations mirror recent successful athletes' efforts to form independent representative bodies of athletes such as Athleten Deutschland or the The Athletics Association. In the case of athletics, the athletes also protested against a specific change in their sport, the removal of the throwing events from the Diamond League events. Thus, the athlete movement in the modern pentathlon appears to be yet another important case of athletes rising up and organizing to address pressing issues affecting their careers.[40]

CHAPTER 4

Oppression of Athletes' Voices

Transparent and inclusive stakeholder participation in decision-making processes is a crucial element in democratic systems. When the "governed" can influence policy processes, the "government" usually receives much higher approval for their actions. This in turn results in fewer challenges to regulations, decisions, and policies. However, as outlined, the main stakeholders within the sport system, the athletes, have often been excluded from policy processes. This is despite the fact they have no influence on the rules and regulations that directly influence their sporting experiences and, in some cases, even their personal lives. Such a hierarchical system of governance has caused athletes to increasingly challenge and protest, leading to some changes in recent years. As will be shown in this chapter, the activists strongly accuse the UIPM of ignoring and in some cases even censoring the views of athletes, despite public claims to include the athlete community in the decision-making processes. In this vein, the athletes argue that their voices are oppressed.

The severe dissatisfaction with the current processes of athletes' representation can be explained with alternating understandings of the implementation of democratic principles in the organization. The activists' strongly call for a *direct* involvement of athletes in decision-making processes within the federation. They do so by highlighting how the representative democracy system is severely flawed and hinders stakeholder engagement to take effect. This impedes the acceptance of decisions, transparent decision-making, and improved performance of the federation on the whole.

International Level

The activists accuse the UIPM leadership of ignoring and willingly silencing the voices of the athletes. This allegation comes predominantly from the current and recently retired athletes interviewed within the group. The majority of the athletes quoted the perceived silencing of athletes as the main reason to become engaged in the protest activities – clearly outweighing the riding issue. "Decisions are made by officials, there is no publicity and no dialogue with athletes," one current competitor said. If those allegations are proven correct, the UIPM would thereby be found acting in opposition to current trends that sport organizations increasingly recognize the importance of athletes in the governance of the international sport system.[1] NF representatives also acknowledged that the athletes are mainly concerned about their lack of influence and less about the broader governance issues. "Athletes have their mind elsewhere and they are not used to politics," it was explained. Thus, some federations felt a responsibility towards those athletes who are currently active in the sport.

It is vital to affirm that the athletes' community in modern pentathlon has a prehistory in its collective attempts to engage in a dialogue with the UIPM leadership. In 2007, when the UIPM proposed to change the format of shooting and running to a combined event, more than one hundred athletes signed a letter to UIPM President Klaus Schormann opposing the changes. At the time, the athletes reasoned that the change in format would not benefit the development of the sport, more marketing initiatives were

Oppression of Athletes' Voices

necessary, and there had to be a greater dialogue between athletes, coaches, and the UIPM leadership.[2] The initiative had no impact and the changes were implemented after a Congress decision. In fact, in the response letter, the athletes were reminded in the first sentence of the answer that "the athletes do not represent their National Federations."[3] This statement is certainly correct, but its essence strengthens the impression that the athletes are considered at the bottom of the sport's hierarchical order.

Irrespective of the legality of the UIPM Executive Board's initial decision at the end of October 2021 to propose a modern pentathlon format without riding for the 2028 Los Angeles Olympic Games, it is evident that the athlete community was not consulted *before* the decision was made. To many of the interviewed athletes, the lack of athletes' involvement did not come as a surprise. "The UIPM does not respect the athletes or the community," one current athlete complained. A former athlete, who had also had insights into the working procedures of the UIPM Executive Board agreed: "When you are sitting on the Executive, they listen to you but nothing happens. Their decisions are not about the athletes, but only about them. About business, about fame." A current competitor in the sport gave the treatment of athletes at UIPM events as an example. "The difference in treatment is stunning," she said. "They literally provide us with cold fast food in our lunch boxes (...) And you look over at the Executive Board and these guys would drive in in hired Mercedes cars and they would have canapes seating and have organized silver service meals. I mean that is incredible."

Only after the MPADK submitted its legal complaint and athletes voiced their discontent did the UIPM speak with the athletes. UIPM documentation provided at the 2021 Congress also conveys this sequence of events.[4] The UIPM's initial official message to modern pentathletes - via an open letter posted online at the beginning of November 2021 - shows how the UIPM attempted to shield itself against criticism. "Today we communicate the Executive Board's decision to you, with an assurance that you will be centrally involved in this consultation," the press release read. "Without our athletes, our movement would be nothing – and your voices must be heard."[5] The contradictory nature of the statement is obvious. The UIPM speaks about a "decision," i.e. a conclusion or resolution, highlighting that a reversal was not possible. Thus, the UIPM could have only meant an involvement in the consultancy about the new discipline, but not about the decision to remove riding beyond the 2028 Olympic Games.

When the UIPM eventually held an online meeting with the athletes on November 12, 2021, the leadership attempted to carefully steer the narrative, not allowing for an open debate. Participating athletes recalled that they had to submit questions in advance and were only allowed to speak to ask their question. Other than that, they were muted for the entire session. Follow-up questions were not possible at all. When athletes demanded more speaking time in the chat, the UIPM administration disabled the chat function for the majority of the meeting, blaming a technical error. "But it was obvious that they wanted to control our input," a protesting athlete recalled. It was also not a discussion about the issues in horse-riding. As British athlete Samantha Murray told *InsidetheGames*, "they just did not entertain the topic of 'how could we solve equestrian'."[6] One source said: "The only thing we could do was listen. I wanted to speak but they did not give me the word." Another athlete said: "It was not a two-way conversation, but a controlled Q&A. It was just bizarre." Such handling of the meeting mirrors academic accounts on how sport organizations communicate with athletes. Open dialogues are an exception during athletes' meetings with sport leaders. The latter usually set the tone of the meeting with actual concerns of athletes rarely addressed.[7]

It is clear that the UIPM needed to have some control over the meeting in order to allow for a structured debate. However, the degree of control executed in the meeting appears to have been exceeded significantly, and reflects complaints of those questioning the open debate opportunities at the 2021 UIPM Congress.

Importantly, the UIPM - as is the case for the majority of international governing bodies of sport - has its own way of involving athletes in the decision-making processes via its the UIPM AC federation who had a member on the UIPM Executive Board. AC members are nominated by their NFs and athletes vote for them at international events. The elected AC members then vote amongst themselves for a chairperson.

UIPM AC Chair Aya Medany from Egypt, was present at the Executive Board meetings and therefore athletes' representation was ensured in line with the UIPM statutes.[8] Medany must have initially voted for the removal of horse-riding as it was communicated that the decision had been made unanimously. The athletes in the activist group argue that the athletes were not consulted by her before the vote. According to the interviewed athletes, there was not even communication between Medany and the other members of the UIPM AC prior to the Executive Board decision: "Medany consulted nobody from the athlete community about the decision." This appears understandable considering the very short notice of the meeting. One athlete said, however, that he had communicated with Medany after the Executive Board meeting and she informed that she had attempted to vote in the best interest of the sport, trying to save its place on the Olympic programme. Therefore she went with the majority of the Board members. This confirms the above outlined criticism voiced by other researchers about the role of internal ACs in sporting bodies, who are severely restricted in their representative function and power.

It is clear that according to the UIPM statutes Medany was rightfully elected by the athletes to represent their interests and vote on their behalf. However, in such a delicate and transformative topic, it seems inherently important to inform oneself on the general opinion amongst the athletes if one acts as their representative. Ahead of the UIPM Congress vote, Pentathlon United demanded from Medany that she publicly confirmed that she would vote against the drop of riding.[9] This demand remained unanswered, but Medany did come out at the Congress and said that she was against the removal of riding but first and foremost the survival of modern pentathlon had to be secured. This statement is consistent with her opinion voiced in the conversation with the athlete above. According to her, this attitude reflected the opinions of the athletes, who had sent her letters expressing their thoughts.[10]

After the November 2021 Congress, a new UIPM AC started to represent the athletes. Interestingly, the new chair, Yasser Hefny, is again from Egypt. Some athletes were concerned about them being represented by a Egyptian athlete again because Egyptian fellow athletes had reported in athletes' meetings that they could not speak out. Moreover, Egypt also has a member on the UIPM Executive Board. In addition, two athletes highlighted that Hefny had taken on the position as the Egyptian head coach of the sport. As such, they argued, he was employed by the Egyptian UIPM Executive Board member, possibly restricting him to freely speak out. They also had concerns that a coach was representing the athletes' interests. Importantly, while some athletes acknowledged that the athletes had voted Hefny into the UIPM AC, the voting for the chairperson, who votes in the UIPM Executive Board, is an internal process within the UIPM AC. In short, the fact that the one person representing the athletes in the UIPM is a coach and not a current athlete, and works for the federation run by another UIPM Executive Board member, seems questionable.

In response to the public criticism that the athletes were not involved in decision-making processes, the UIPM appointed "10 Olympic pentathletes" to the new 5th Discipline Working Group in December 2021.[11] However, only four of those athletes are currently still active, five of the "athletes" ended their careers more than ten years ago. Thus, what looks on first view like an equal balance between sport administrators and athletes appears to be paying lip service to the demand for athletes' representation. Moreover, three of the four athletes on the working group are members of the UIPM Athletes' AC with restricted possibilities to independently defend the athletes' interests. "The athlete representation on the working group, I mean, it's a joke," one source said. The person continued: "This is more to, again they use the rhetoric we formed a committee, we engaged athletes, and this is the outcome." In connection with such protests are many athletes concerned that individual Executive Board members claim they represent the athletes because they had been competitors themselves in the past. For example, UIPM Treasurer John Helmick argued in a video call that the UIPM Executive Board thinks "we are the athletes" because many former Olympians sit on the board.[12] It is easy to understand that currently active athletes are irritated by such statements when they are trying to push for a participatory system. They share very little characteristics with those claiming to represent the athletes.

In addition, all members of the 5th Discipline Working Group had to sign non-disclosure agreements prior to the first meeting, severely restricting an open exchange between the athlete community and its representatives about potential replacements for horse-riding. Therefore, on paper, the UIPM might be able to satisfy the demand, voiced by the IOC Sport Director McConnell, that any decision needs to have credibility from the side of the athletes.[13] However, the interviewed athletes collectively argue that the majority of the athlete community is disregarded in the process. "No one has spoken with me, yet. And no other athlete I know has been consulted either," said one athlete after the working group had already met in mid-January 2022. In fairness, after the initial 5th Discipline Commission meeting, the athletes' representatives began to organize exchanges with athletes. However, rather than allowing the athletes to appoint several spokespersons, selected athletes were invited to speak on the topic. Some of the athletes were junior competitors with very little experience on the international scene. Joe Choong, the current Olympic champion and an outspoken activist, was absent from the list of invitees, and so was Kate French, the gold medal winner in the women's event at the 2020 Tokyo Olympic Games.

The athletes reported another example of how the UIPM leadership attempted to interfere with the claimed autonomy of athletes that occurred in mid-December 2021. Following the continuing calls for their voices to be heard, the IOC Athletes' Commission invited the UIPM AC to speak about the ongoing issues with IOC staff members. Pentathlon United representative Kate Allenby was also invited to participate - but, crucially, not to speak - during the call. What was communicated as an independent opportunity for athletes to have their own questions answered by the IOC, took place with official UIPM leadership involvement as UIPM General Secretary Fang participated in the call. Therewith, the UIPM leadership could oversee the discussions, with athletes potentially afraid to speak out freely. Such a line of action reflects processes in other sport organizations, in which the leadership controls "athlete involvement" and has led to calls for athlete bodies independent from sport organizations.[14]

Finally, the athletes reported that there were major concerns amongst the UIPM leadership that the athletes could not be controlled. Therefore, members of the UIPM Executive Board allegedly undertook efforts to spy on the communication between the athletes. When in November 2021 the first *WhatsApp* and *Telegram* groups formed, information was forwarded to the UIPM leadership. After going through the registered mobile phone numbers, some athletes found out that UIPM Executive Board members had taken on fake names and pretended to be athletes in order to be included in the group chats. Screenshots verifying such subterfuge attempts have been provided.

In summary, the interviewed athletes felt that their voices remain ignored in the ongoing discussions on the future of modern pentathlon. Some athletes were not surprised about the situation. "I knew that in sport, the athlete is the last person the leaders listen to," one athlete claimed. Regarding the removal of horse-riding, athletes were - like all other stakeholders outside the UIPM Executive Board - not actively consulted at all. This is despite the fact an overwhelming majority of the athletes spoke out publicly against the change. In the process of finding a new discipline, athlete involvement appears to be at most symbolic. It is certainly difficult to include all stakeholders at all times in decision-making. In fact, that is why organizations vote for executive working groups to take over those tasks. However, the mechanisms revealed here indicate that there is strong resistance to include the group of athletes into decision-making at any level.

Taken together with the suspicions that a strategy for a replacement discipline is already in place, athletes rightly consider taking more severe action. At various times in the process, the UIPM leadership did not only ignore the athletes' voices but also undertook active attempts to silence them, for example through restricting speaking time, spying on their communication, and seemingly instructing representatives to abstain from consulting the athletes' community.

National level

Another aspect previously receiving little academic attention emerged during the interviews with the athletes. In claiming that they do not feel represented by the UIPM AC, some turned to their NFs for support. In some cases, NF representatives backed the athletes, but in other cases, athletes did not find any support. "It is not possible to speak with our leaders," one athlete complained. In one country, athletes repeatedly addressed the NF's athletes committee but their messages remained unanswered, showing the flaws of the representation model on the national level, too.

One federation, which is represented by an individual on the UIPM Executive Board, even reached out to the athletes directly to declare that the decision to drop riding was final. This was despite the fact that the pentathlon community in this country had not been questioned whether it actually backed this decision. The athletes were told that any protests could be damaging to their careers, an attempt to choke off potential disruptions and restrict freedom of speech. If proven correct, such behavior would seriously put into question those NF leaders' mandate to act as representatives of their home federations. In one country, the athletes are now attempting to demonstrate the backing for horse-riding through the creation of a survey amongst all modern pentathlon participants, a survey which should have been facilitated by those making the vote on behalf of their national modern pentathlon community.

According to information provided by activists discussed during an athlete meeting, several NFs told their elite competitors in January that they would be removed from the national team if they protested the horse-riding removal. As a result, the athletes were scared to speak out and participate in any activities through which they could be identified by name. One athlete recalled the statement of another athlete, who reported that she would be "punished" if she expressed her opinion. Another athlete reported that a sport administrator with a double role in the UIPM and a NF spoke in an "aggressive" tone with young athletes, warning them: "if you talk a lot about this, it will not be good for your career." One athlete explained how the federations can indirectly prevent the athletes from speaking out: "The NFs employs the head coaches who are financially dependent on the federation. In this way, the NFs can dictate which athletes should be selected for the international competitions." Another stated: "I am scared that they will cut me off." It is noteworthy that many of the federations that allegedly prevent athletes from speaking out are represented on the UIPM Executive Board. Without doubt, such an instruction contradicts the athletes' right to free speech and must therefore be considered an abuse of their human rights.

To be clear, such measures were not taken by all NFs. Some also took the athletes' opinion on board and changed their original standpoint on horse-riding. One athlete reported: "when the athletes spoke out, the federation took a 180 degree turn." Such a change of direction appears to have been more the exception than the rule.

In another, verifiable case of ignoring athletes' voices, athletes sent a petition to USA Pentathlon Multisport (USAPM) asking to vote against the removal of horse-riding. The petition included 252 signatures and a letter with 54 athletes' signatures. "This reflects around 99% of all elite athletes," one individual explained. A survey by USAPM's own athlete committee also showed a large majority of athletes to keep horse riding in the sport.[15] However, USAPM representatives allegedly voted for the removal of the equestrian event.[16] According to the activists, their actions constitute a violation of the USAPM's laws as per section 7.2. of its bylaws.[17]

Within this context, it is necessary to remind readers about the fears previously mentioned by Russian competitors about political consequences if they speak out against their federation in public. Economic aspects were also mentioned by athletes. One interviewee said that some athletes receive funding from the UIPM to compete internationally. As a result, those athletes do not consider themselves to be in a position to speak out freely. Similarly, in many countries the athletes are employed by their military and fear severe consequences if they make their voices known.

Some UIPM leaders also fell back on the well-known rhetoric that they had themselves been elite athletes in the sport and therefore represented the athletes.[18] However, first of all those individuals are on the Executive Board to represent the federation rather than athletes. Furthermore, they have been away from competition for several decades and certainly do not share many characteristics with current competitors - particularly not when the sport has changed so much in recent times.

Without doubt, the athletes' protests are in line with the current Zeitgeist within international sport in which active athletes are demanding a greater say in decision-making processes. However, the accusations raised by the modern pentathlon community go far beyond that. Athletes' voices are at best ignored by the UIPM leadership, at worst actively suppressed. The UIPM's rhetoric to openly listen to the athletes' community misleads the public in a significant way. Rather, there is good reason to assume that the modern pentathlon athletes appear to be, to borrow the description of scholar Helen Lenskyj, "pawns in an exploitative system," with little if any recognition through the UIPM leadership. Any inclusion of athletes seems to be controlled by those in power. The referral to the UIPM AC members is flawed if this body does not act in the interests of the majority of athletes. The athletes, to whom the leaders own their privilege of overseeing a sport,[19] are largely disregarded. Importantly, not only the UIPM leadership but also sport officials in NFs appear to have abused their positions of power here.

The athletes argue that the UIPM leadership does not make deliberate attempts to reach out to the athlete community, maintaining that so-called "athletes first" policies are only paying lip service to public criticism and the demands of the IOC. As such, they see a severe marginalization of the non-elites - the athletes - in the power structures of the sport.

The presented case of the restricted possibilities for the UIPM AC to represent the athletes mirrors the general situation of athletes' bodies that are integrated in the institutional framework of sport organizations. For example, the athlete commissions' press statements have to be approved by the governing bodies before they are published as the members on the committees are first and foremost representatives of the institution. As such, they do not act like trade unions which aim to protect workers from their employers, even though sport organizations publicly imply that this is the case. Some might argue that the athletes accept representation through an athletes' commission as they are voting for their representatives. However, starting from the assumption that the athletes are disempowered and lack the necessary resources to obtain knowledge about the commission system, they are left with little choice. This imbalance must be revealed to the athletes. Thus, the knowledge gained from this study is significant for the athletes' community and wider protest movement.

CHAPTER 5

Disregard for Principles of Governance

The strong calls from modern pentathlon athletes for involvement in decision-making need to be contextualized with their claims about the UIPM misgovernance. For example, one source claimed: "The UIPM has not kept pace with modern standards for good governance." It is therefore vital to discuss those accusations against the background of good governance principles and contrast the accusations with the activists own perceptions on sports governance.

In this chapter, the activists' accusations regarding UIPM leadership will be contextualized by drawing on the definitions and concepts of the *Sports Governance Observer* (SGO). In comparison with other sports-internal governance instruments, the SGO framework has the distinct advantage that it has been developed outside the system of organized sport and therefore constitutes an independent benchmarking tool to assess the performance of sport organizations.[1] The SGO has been applied to assess the governance of IFs in previous studies.[2]

The good governance dimensions of democracy, transparency, and accountability will be discussed in the following as the activists argue that those three principles have significantly been violated. At this stage, readers are reminded about the two key approaches of this study. First, the majority of the respondents were active and recently retired athletes and the voiced criticism reflects their perception of the governance of modern pentathlon. The statements must therefore be contextualized with the perceived marginalization of athletes in decision-making as discussed in the previous chapter. The athletes' acknowledged lack of power is the starting point for the analysis. Second, this study does not survey the UIPM's rules and regulations such as governance observers. It attempts to expose the "real-life governance" and organizational cultures in the federation behind the procedural prerequisites for good governance. The SGO therefore serves as a structural and normative framework rather than as an assessment tool of the good governance dimensions.

Democracy

Democratic processes within sport organizations refer to free and competitive elections, involvement of all actors in decision-making processes, as well as open debates in an organization's main forums such as working groups and general assemblies. Research and NGOs engaged in good governance studies argue that the adherence to principles of democracy will lead to more effective policies generated through stakeholder involvement in decision-making. In addition, more solutions will be generated and individuals will be motivated to act in the interest of an organization if they are continuously challenged in their policy-making.[3]

The athletes interviewed as well as other activists claim that the current and past UIPM leadership disregarded democratic processes, which in turn allowed certain individuals to remain in power and establish a regime which was uncontestable in practice. Therefore, they call for a turnover of the current leadership and the installation of a new governance system that focuses on direct involvement of the entire modern pentathlon community.

Terms in Office

The limitation of terms in office is considered to be a key element of good governance in sport. Sunder Katwala, in his groundbreaking work on democratizing global sport, claimed in 2000 that presidencies of more than eight years (two terms) might result in an unhealthy concentration of power.[4] More recently, the President of the Association of Summer Olympic International Federations (ASOIF) Francesco Ricci Bitti went public with a plea to all IFs to introduce term limits in an attempt to better the governance in their organizations.[5] Without term limitations, individuals in power can enjoy advantages over challengers due to their seniority in the position. Moreover, those in power are gradually losing touch with their communities and therewith properly contested elections prevent a concentration of power and contribute to the generation of new strategies.[6]

For almost all activists interviewed, the UIPM's current struggles are linked to the long-term regime of current president Klaus Schormann and a close circle of individuals around him. The lack of change in leadership, the activists argue, hindered innovation from taking place and limited the sport's development. This is despite the fact that Schormann did initiate reforms such as the introduction of the combined event and the laser run. "He took over during a difficult time," one former athlete acknowledged. The UIPM was not in a good shape at the beginning of the 1990s, some activists explained. Blaming the lack of vision of Schormann's predecessors, they state that at the time of Schormann's take-over a problematic organizational culture was already in place: one that did not value good governance principles. Yet, whilst the UIPM would not be an exception of an international governing body of sport with problematic leadership cultures during the 1990s,[7] the activists criticize the continuation of the problems today, decades later. "He brought in a bit of fresh air. But he actually turned into something much worse," one individual argued. Another source said: "There is no new blood in the leadership. It is the same blood every time and this hinders the innovation in our sport. There is only change when there is a problem." In other words, the activists link what they perceive as reactive policies to the long duration of the current leadership.

The activists claim that Schormann's lengthy presidency allowed him to manipulate federations and individuals to make decisions according to his wishes: "Having been in power for nearly thirty years, there's a web cast out from Monaco that spreads around an awful lot of the world. And it has been spread cleverly." Many interviewees pointed towards the Congress' decision to remove horse-riding as evidence. "We had four weeks to prepare for Congress and managed to get 15 people to vote against removing the riding. He has had 30 years, 28 years, to weave that web around the world to influence people to win the vote or get the votes that he did, however he got them." The activists accuse Schormann of having set up a small group of people over which he exerts full control. "Klaus [Schormann] always wants yes men around him. You have to whisper kind words in praise of him to be in his good," one insider claimed. Schormann himself considers the fact that there are no alternative candidates to him an approval of his success. In 2012, he stated in an interview: "I organized it in a way that my work was impressive and therefore no one thought he could contest against me and do it better."[8] Schormann definitely acts within the UIPM statutes here. However, the activists focus on the invisible background mechanisms and exposing that the power in the federation is centered around a few leaders.

It is undeniable that several individuals on the current UIPM Executive Board have played key roles in the governance of the sport for a very long time. For example, I was recently astonished to find a brochure from 1999 in the archive of *The Stark Center for Physical Culture and Sports*, in which many of the individuals that are still currently leading the federation were already featured in articles over two decades prior.[9] UIPM Vice-President Joël Bouzou has been in his current position since 2012 and acted as UIPM General Secretary before. UIPM Vice-President Juan Antonio Samaranch Jr. has been a UIPM Executive Board member since 1984 and has been vice-president since 1996.[10] UIPM Treasurer John Helmick has held several positions within the UIPM leadership since 1993. Therefore, there is reason to believe that open contests for leadership positions cannot realistically be held. Rather, the long-established, closely-knit network would have enabled the UIPM leadership to create a culture of backdoor dealing for almost three decades. One former UIPM official provided an example on how she became involved in prior decision-making without consultation of the broader modern pentathlon community: "All these things were decided (...) and then we go to Congress meetings and basically just everyone else was there like to dress the room but all the decisions had already been made." Comparing such accounts of backdoor decision-making to the handling of the removal of horse-riding and the introduction of the 90-minutes format, give reason to assume that such cultures have remained in place.

Certainly, the UIPM is not the only governing body of sport in which a leader has lasted more than a decade. Comparative studies have highlighted that there is a monopolization of power within sport's governing bodies because of missing term limits.[11] Consequently, many IF leaders are, scholars Lincoln Allison and Alan Tomlinson argue, "in terms of longevity, (...) more like dictators."[12] As a result, Allison and Tomlinson continue, "[sport] leadership has shown distinct messianic characteristics," considering themselves as "unique and indispensable embodiment[s] of the movement."[13]

At this point, it is important to mention that a few activists also made bold statements, falling back on comparisons that they could hardly justify. For example, one activist argued: "They are not prepared to give away even a cent of power. They want to be treated like kings, but their only goal is to stay in power, not to develop the sport." Whilst the evidence does not allow for a judgment whether staying in power is the *only* goal of the leadership, the quote illustrates the anger and emotions that drive some of the athletes. It is therefore important to carefully dissect the statements of the activists.

Taken together, even though the UIPM has democratic principles in place, regulated through its statutes, the activists claim that there is no actual possibility for them to be implemented. According to them, Schormann's long-term leadership has led to dependencies and power structures that do not allow for a real challenge to his presidency. If proven correct, such claims indicate that the modern pentathlon community is severely restricted in putting individuals and underrepresented groups into power through democratic elections. Academic perspectives also refute Schormann's own claim that the voters automatically decide once someone is "out-dated."[14]

Open Debates

In an alleged violation of the democracy principle of good governance that calls for open debates, the activists further accuse the UIPM leadership of shutting down debates and of selectively awarding speaking rights at the 2021 UIPM Congress. The setup of having some members of the Executive Board physically present in Monaco whereas all other Congress participants had to attend virtually supported such a controlling environment. It is argued that the representatives of the federations which had openly criticized the leadership prior to Congress were singled out for such restrictive measures. "The Brits told me that they could hear everyone but Denmark, Sweden, and Finland very well," one Congress participant claimed. The MPADK President Benny Elmann-Larsen publicly stated such concerns, too. The process of the Congress was "grotesque" and "no debate possible," he said in an interview published in France.[15] The activists' perceptions are in stark contrast to the UIPM's defense on the back of the force majeure decision that the Congress "should be a good place to discuss and clarify these matters and hopefully render this dispute moot."[16] Whilst staging online debates, specifically with a high number of participants, is always a challenge, restricting participants to speak out on this significant change to the sport and not allowing for open discussions, would act against the guidance provided by ASOIF for holding virtual general assemblies.[17] As we have seen, awarding only selected individuals with speaking rights also occurred in the UIPM's meetings with athletes, raising suspicions of a pattern by the UIPM leadership.

Importantly, most interviewed individuals acknowledged that the UIPM did not directly violate any constitutional rules. "The 2021 Congress was a brilliantly stage-managed piece of theater by the Executive Board. (...) It was designed to have just enough discussion to avoid the allegation of no discussion. It played perfectly on the difficulties for national federations to coordinate as a block. (...) It was manipulated in the extreme." Other examples from the 2021 Congress that the activists brought up in the interviews were procedural mistakes. These include adding an agenda item the day before without informing the participants, and allowing a UIPM lawyer to speak against the *force majeure* allegations. Thus, at the very least, the claims demonstrate the discrepancy between regulations in place at the UIPM and the reality of those regulations being played out, or misused as the athletes claim.

Another insight shared by two interviewees further highlights how leading UIPM officials act behind the scenes to pressure voters. Two individuals reported independently from each other that following the UIPM President's re-election at the congress, Schormann sent an email to a member federation that had allegedly voted against him, demanding that this NF's leaders should back his leadership and get their leadership in order. Such behavior demonstrates that the UIPM President is prepared to reprimand those who did not support him, attempting to break down potential resistance despite the fact that it is legitimate to demonstrate discontent via voting choices.

The activist group suggests that in the current environment of international sport, such organizational cultures will lead to the UIPM losing credibility. "They've lost their way. We need to get back the respect of a lot of these key stakeholders like the IOC, (...) there a lot of good people there who realize that the organizations have to be open, have to be transparent, have to be about inclusiveness and all the rest of it. And you can only do that if you are honest with everybody you deal with." Thus, the activists appear to put a lot of trust into the IOC and it's more recent dealings with mis-management in other sport organizations.

***

Whilst the UIPM's regulations reflect transparency principles, the reality of decision-making inside the federation appears to be a highly secretive and pressurized environment. This finding is in alignment with the UIPM's alleged treatment of athletes' voices as outlined in the previous chapter. Thus, the lack of open debates runs through the entire sport and not only affects the organizational level, but the entire modern pentathlon community. This is in contrast to the activists' demands for open provision of information and justifications for actions from the leadership. Such lack of responsiveness by the UIPM leadership, which is linked to its secure place in power severely reduces the activists' confidence in the leadership, and is directly linked to the accountability issues discussed in the next section.

Accountability

According to the SGO, the "internal accountability and control" principles "refers to both the separation of powers in the organization's governance structure and a system of rules and procedures that ensures that staff and officials comply with internal rules and norms. Upholding the accountability principle is crucial in a democratic system, as it allows those affected by policies to hold the elected officials accountable for their actions. The principle is violated if the voters, here the NFs, cannot hold those in power - the UIPM leadership in this instance - accountable for their actions. Even with accountability regulations and checks and balances mechanisms in place, accountability can be severely threatened if the voters have no real possibility to challenge the leadership. Such a scenario increases the possibility of power imbalances, abuses of power, and unethical behavior. The athlete-led protesters accuse the UIPM leadership of exactly that.

Voting Mechanism and Clientelism

Political systems, but also the power relationship within sport organizations, can be undermined by clientelism - violating the accountability principle.[18] In short, clientelism is the allocation of private goods or favors by a patron/leader to his clients in return for favors - usually in the form of votes - to manifest the power role of the patron/leader.[19] Such a relationship weakens the democracy within an organization as it does not allow for openly contested elections. The issue is closely linked to the debate on voting systems within IFs. All but seven Olympic IFs employ so-called one-nation-one-vote systems that are thought to threaten the integrity of sport by facilitating corruption and vote-buying. A study from 2022, of those seven IFs working with a weighted voting system, shows that they put more emphasis on the involvement of member federations in the sport and the promotion of good governance.[20]

The activists argue that the UIPM's one-country-one-vote system in place has been exploited for clientelist purposes despite the statutes adhering to democratic principles. Indeed, whilst the large majority of athletes were quarantined from decision-making in all parts of the process, the NFs had the possibility to vote against the Executive Board decision at the 2021 UIPM Congress, held virtually. According to some activists, herein lies one of the structural issues in the federation: "We should change the voting system," one claimed, echoing calls by some researchers that sport organization's might consider the establishment of a system that acknowledges the greater involvement of larger NFs.[21]

The UIPM has significantly raised its efforts to admit new members in the past three decades. In 2012, UIPM President Schormann proudly noted in an interview: "When I started, we had 63 nations. Now we will have 130 in the coming weeks - and others are in the waiting loop." Interestingly, he continued, "paper corps and those things are not possible because of our statutes and every federation must have athletes who at least participate in biathle."[22] The UIPM now boasts 129 federations, but the activists question how many of those federations are actively engaged in the sport. "From 2016 the UIPM president started recruiting new NFs with no modern pentathlon tradition or basic possibilities for practicing the sport," one source informed in writing. The source continued: "It became clear that the congress probably never any more would be able to win a vote that the president didn't support."

This raises an important question about the UIPM's internationalization attempts. The IOC demands that sports included in the Olympic programme be practiced as widely as possible. One measurement tool for international participation is the number of recognized NFs. The activists recognize the need to address this issue, but claim that internationalization is exploited by the UIPM to remain in power: "on the one level, increasing the members is a defense strategy, on the other hand the level of influence those nations can take is staggering." The activists claim that many NFs were forced into voting for the horse-riding removal due to dependencies on the current leadership. In some cases, the activist claimed, the NFs are not even recognized by their National Olympic Committees (NOCs) and only exist on paper. In order to establish full transparency, "it is looking at those nations, and seeing how they are funded and how they are created, and where they are influenced," one interviewee highlighted.

The majority of such criticism focuses on NFs from the African continent. Of the UIPM's current 127 NFs, 30 are from the African continent. Yet their participation in the sport, including in a peripheral sense, is limited. In 2021, at a qualifying event for the Youth Olympic Games contested without horse-riding for organizational reasons specifically to allow for *more* participation, only four NFs participated. This highlights not only that horse-riding might not be the only obstacle those countries are facing in the sport, but it certainly provides evidence for the lack of engagement by those NFs. Taken together African NFs hold almost a fourth of the UIPM General Assembly's voting power, but questions must be asked whether their severely limited participation justifies such a high degree of influence. Importantly, this is not to say that African federations should not participate in modern pentathlon and other sports of the UIPM sporting pyramid, but to highlight that an inclusion into the UIPM must be tied to serious involvement and interest in the sport.

And the allegations do not stop here as some activists claimed that there are NFs which only exist on paper. Pentathlon United publicly questioned the recognition status of 27 NFs. One activist conducted a simple research on all NOC websites of modern pentathlon federations and found that the several NOCs did not list an official modern pentathlon federation. Indeed, just one spot check undertaken for the purpose of this research revealed that at least one NF participated in the voting at the 2021 UIPM Congress that is not recognized by its NOC. The NOC confirmed the absent recognition status in writing. There are further inconsistencies. For example, the Namibian Modern Pentathlon Federation is still listed on the UIPM website as a member even though they have allegedly informed the UIPM leadership that their NF was dissolved.[23]

Yet, the criticism of the activist group does not only address those NFs that no longer exist (or never did). A few interviewed individuals also claim that many NFs are not involved in the sport at all, despite official recognition. "They only get something through the backdoor but they are not involved in the sport," one activist claimed. It is certainly correct that competitors from many nations do not participate in the full modern pentathlon programme with all five disciplines and the lack of access to horse-riding opportunities is a particular concern for them. For example, the Uganda Modern Pentathlon Federation in a support letter to the UIPM Executive Board's decision, reasoned: "Horse riding is very expensive and this has hindered us as a federation to grow the sport considering the logistics required. Horses are rare to find in [our] country and them being athletes of the sport, it becomes hard to groom them considering the requirements."[24]

The activists argue that some federations - specifically those not extensively engaged in the sport - have been encouraged to become UIPM members solely for the purpose of supporting the existing power structures. "The leadership has become fixated on securing survival through creating all these federations globally," one activist argued. "Some federations were created by UIPM officials," another one said, indicating that rather than supporting the development of the sport on the ground, individuals from the UIPM leadership sought to create federations to maintain power. Those federations are under [the] control of the UIPM leadership, the group explains. One interviewed individual said: "when they [member federations without active involvement in modern pentathlon] come to a congress, the leadership can say what they should vote for because they can control the allocation of development money." The suspicions amongst the activists even go as far as they believe an email address of an NF might directly lead to a UIPM Executive Board member not of that country.

There are also direct financial dependencies of African member federations to the UIPM that emerged shortly before the 2021 Congress. In mid-November 2021, of the thirty member federations from the African continent, twenty-seven had not paid their UIPM membership fees. According to written exchanges, the only exceptions were Egypt, Madagascar, and South Africa.[25] The African confederation usually pays the fees for its members, but this had not been the case for 2021. Therefore, the UIPM - by referring to the ongoing pandemic - paid the membership fees for the remaining members, thereby effectively enabling those federations to vote at the 2021 Congress. This can be considered a solidaric move, however, it also raised suspicions amongst the activists. For example, it adds weight to statements in which athletes accuse the UIPM leadership of exploiting financial dependencies. "Certain federations receive money from the UIPM, and they need that move to survive. Therefore the UIPM always has a financial reason to use as leverage in exchange for votes." one athlete said. Clearly, only an independent, open investigation can reveal whether such severe accusations are correct.

Single UIPM Executive Board members seem to be open about their support for less financially powerful federations. In the accompanying document for the 2021 UIPM Congress, UIPM Vice President Viacheslav Aminov from Russia stated: "I am very friendly with the President of the South American Confederation Jorge Salas. His activities and his impact on the development of Modern Pentathlon in South America are impressive. Some years ago I decided that I will assist him in all his initiations and I am helping this region *from my own resources* with different equipment: fencing and shooting."[26] This statement clearly indicates a clientelist system. If Aminov indeed uses his private money to support economically weaker member federations, it might be in their interest to keep him and the current leadership in power. On this basis, the activists argue that the UIPM leadership has created a system through which it can reward its main voters like clients, and, as noted by other researchers, "it is ultimately those who control the votes who matter." One athlete revealed that the NF's leadership of the country had voted for the removal as follows: "My federation was scared that the UIPM leadership will not help it anymore if they had voted no."

Without question, the UIPM leadership would not be the first IF leadership to run a clientelist system. Both the former President of the International Federation of Associate Football, Joseph Blatter, and World Athletics' long-time leader Primo Nebiolo persuaded Global South member federations to vote for them and rewarded them with access to development funds.[27] In 2015, the Danish newspaper *Politiken* revealed that the International Handball Federation recruited members without any real connections to the sport in an attempt to consolidate power and make them dependent on the IHF leadership.[28] Finally, after a vote at the FEI General Assembly to decide about the continuation of three-member teams in equestrian sport for the 2024 Olympic Games - with alleged negative impacts on horse welfare - the International Jumping Riders Club found that less than 10% of the countries voting in favor of the three-rider format had ever competed at the Olympic Games.[29]

However, whereas football and athletics are practiced globally by millions of individuals, modern pentathlon is a small sport that struggles to find participants. This limitation causes the UIPM to struggle to fulfill the IOC's universality criteria. In order to address this challenge, the current UIPM leadership appears to work with NFs that only exist on paper and are tenuously engaged in the sport - if at all. With this strategy, it kills two birds with one stone as those federations want to keep the leadership in power, which makes it barely possible for the federations with real interests in the sport to challenge the leadership. This issue is also a result of the one-federation-one-vote system, whose flaws have been noted by scholars previously. Whilst this system secures equal representation, it fosters corruption and vote buying.[30] In line with such assumptions, several sources suggested the introduction of weighted votes to improve the democratic quality of the UIPM decision-making processes.

In addition, the claim is made that the voting procedures on the national level are also influenced by individuals to remain in power, violating democratic principles. Some of the activists reported that in one NF, the federation listed family members, co-workers, and friends on the list of eligible voters for the executive board. The activists argued that this was done to maintain a majority.

In short, the activists claim that the UIPM leadership established clientelist relationships with many member federations and attempted to expand the number of members to make it difficult for the international modern pentathlon community to challenge the leadership. Ironically, when Denmark challenged the UIPM on the force majeure issue, UIPM Vice-President Joël Bouzou hit back in a public interview, stating: "These Federations are the first to contest, but they organize very few international competitions and very few with horse riding. (...) And when you see the mass of athletes, some have so few that they better shut up."[31] Similarly, UIPM General Secretary Shiny Fang in the 2021 UIPM Congress attacked the NFs from Sweden and Denmark about their claim to represent the athletes. In the Congress minutes it is noted:

> "SGF (Secretary Generale Fang) asked where their athletes are since in the past decades, the data in UIPM major MP events shows that there were no Swedish MP athletes, male or female, and just one female MP athlete from Denmark who competed in 2019. She stressed she would like to know what the problems and the issues of their nations are to develop the sport and underlines that the UIPM would like to help them with any issues on that matter, but if those nations are claiming to represent their athletes, again, please let us know where they are."[32]

Whilst it might be correct that Denmark's participation in the sport is somewhat limited, it is the majority of "smaller" member federations that maintain the power balance and are exposed by those currently in power.

Summarizing this argument of the activist group also produces an important message for the participating athletes. As outlined above, modern pentathletes' voices appear to be ignored in the decision-making of their federation. This is bad enough in itself. However, if the decisions that affect their careers are in fact made by individuals and federations, who are not engaged in the sport at all, athletes have the right to call for considerable changes. To be perfectly clear, the activists and this research do not promote the view that federations with little engagement in the sport should not be members of the UIPM. However, if they are *only* on the international governing body to support the current leadership to remain in power and there is no development work to support the promotion of the sport in the country, the system is considerably flawed and a distortion of democratic principles.

Conflicts of Interest and a Done Deal?

Disregard for accountability also stands at the core of another claim by the activists. Some interviewees contended that Schormann and his allies had already picked a replacement sport before the decision to drop horse-riding and that their intentions reveal strong conflicts of interest. Indeed, Schorman told German broadcaster *ARD* already on November 9 - a little over a week after the initial Executive Board decision - that the leadership had selected a new sport but did not want to reveal it yet. "It will not be cycling," was the only additional insight he provided at the time.[33] One week later, Schormann had to backpedal. He publicly praised the constructive proposals coming from the pentathlon community and promised to consider the different suggested options.[34] However, with the initial statement on the selection of a replacement sport made early in the process, the suspicion remained that at the very least talks had taken place about a specific discipline. Of course, the leadership of a sporting organization (like any other business) has to target modernization and innovation, and be prepared for external challenges. Yet, the severity of the significance of the seizure coupled with utter silence about a potential horse-riding removal, would have required open communication about the strategies developed by the leadership.

The activists further claim that the composition of the 5th Discipline Working Group was arranged based on the intended outcome of the process, and not in the best interest of the sport. When speaking with several activists throughout December 2021, there was a constant refrain from the activists that obstacle racing would replace horse-riding. Obstacle racing includes events such as Spartan Races and Tough Mudders and has enjoyed rising participation numbers in recent years.[35] On December 23, Ukrainian modern pentathlon athlete Pavel Tymoshchenko came public with this suggestion, posting in a Facebook group his opinion that obstacle course racing would replace horse-riding.[36]

Importantly, Tymoshchenko claimed that UIPM Executive Board member Rob Stull was also a board member of World Obstacle Racing (OCR), the governing body for the sport. Stull joined the UIPM Executive Board in 2016 as the representative of the North American, Central American and Caribbean Confederation of Modern Pentathlon. Suspiciously, Stull had been removed from the OCR website after the post and he also deleted the information on obstacle racing from his *LinkedIn* profile, as claimed by individuals from the activists. This fueled the activists' speculations. Moreover, it is evident that UIPM President Schormann undertook several visits to obstacle course racing events from 2016 onwards.[37] In fact, there had already been an attempt to involve obstacle racing into the Olympic version of the modern pentathlon before. When the UIPM proposed to include a mixed relay into the Olympic Games in 2017, it suggested that obstacle course racing would become a part of the laser-run discipline.[38] The UIPM had trialed this format at a demonstration event during the 2017 World Cup in Los Angeles. Different perceptions of the format were already evident at the time. The UIPM considered the introduction of the obstacles as "interesting" and "spectacular" in a press release that does not include any athlete statements.[39] In contrast, an interviewed athlete characterized the event as a "disaster."

Members of the activist group pointed out that Stull's alleged double involvement in obstacle course racing and modern pentathlon was a conflict of interest, and a violation of Article 4 of the UIPM Statutes. Similarly, an athlete from the United States highlighted that individual NFs might not be neutral in the process. In the United States, USA Pentathlon MultiSport (USAPM) serves as the national governing body for modern pentathlon. The governing body for obstacle course racing, USA Obstacle Course Racing is a member of the USAPM. Finally, the interests in joining forces are mutual. Joe De Sena, the founder of the Spartan Race and a key figure in the obstacle race scene, already voiced his "Olympic dream" in 2016.[40]

One athlete revealed that an UIPM Executive Board member informed him and other members of the national modern pentathlon community in early 2022 that UIPM President Schormann had made links with OCR already in 2016. In a video made available for this research, the UIPM Executive Board member said that Schormann already after the 2016 Rio Olympic Games created a secret working group to search for an alternative to riding. It emerged then, according to the UIPM Executive Board member, that it would be a type of Spartan Race or Crossfit. Without doubt, such revelations strongly fuel the activist group's assumption that, first, steps had been taken long before the Executive Board decision in October 2021 and, second, that a specific sport form has already been favored (or even picked) despite the ongoing processes to find a new discipline.

Of course, the attraction of obstacle racing to the UIPM is understandable. Not only is obstacle racing enjoying a consistent increase in participants, it also commands a global following while appealing to a young audience. One could also make the argument that the barrier to entry to obstacle racing is significantly lower than to horse riding. Obstacle racing also ties into the idea of the modern pentathlete portraying the complete soldier, as advocated by Pierre de Coubertin. In fact, when the UIPM proposed the inclusion of obstacle course racing in the mixed relay in 2017, a press release already highlighted the "strong ties to the historical traditions of the Modern Pentathlon."[41] A modern pentathlon including obstacle running would further closely resemble the military pentathlon, consisting of shooting, obstacle running, obstacle swimming, throwing, and cross-country running.[42] Interestingly, it was introduced as an updated version of the modern pentathlon in 1946 with its inventors arguing that many of the skills needed in the Olympic modern pentathlon were outdated.

It is also important to highlight that there is nothing wrong, in principle, with an executive body attempting to broaden the network of the federation and working with external partners. This appears to be a normal and future-orientated strategy. The UIPM also reported about some of the UIPM president's activities with OCR and linked disciplines, and individual UIPM member federation were consulted about a potential institutionalization of those links. The problem arises once there is no full transparency.

However, whilst from an UIPM perspective, it might be lucrative and logical to introduce obstacle course racing as the fifth discipline, the interviewed athletes strongly disagreed. They did not consider obstacle course racing an adequate replacement for horse-riding. It is a "bad idea, because it is another physical sport, it is not technical, not what pentathlon is about," one activist claimed. Another interviewee said that an introduction of obstacle course racing would be particularly tough for the older athletes. "Pentathlon requires a lot of practice and this would change the entire dynamics of the sport. A different energy, and a different body are needed to compete in obstacle course racing," one experienced athlete explained.

At this point some readers might conclude that no matter what suggestion is put forward to modernize the sport, the interviewed athletes will stubbornly reject them and stick with the traditional form of the modern pentathlon. Those readers are reminded about the concrete reform proposals to the riding discipline that the activist group proposes. In fact, the athletes are open to changes to the sport and certainly see the need for modernization. For example, one activist said, "I am not married to the horses. If I would see the benefits of a change in discipline, I would support it." Some athletes also stated that their careers would be secured if riding would not be replaced at all but modern pentathlon would continue with four disciplines only. "At least then we could continue with their careers after 2024," one athlete said. Thus, many of them are willing to make concessions, but decided to stand their ground due to the leadership problems they identified.

★★★

In summary, the activists make two main accusations. First, some individuals assert that individuals on the UIPM Executive Board, including UIPM President Schormann, did not report their activities aimed at the inclusion of obstacle course racing. The UIPM leadership is therefore accused of a violation of its responsibility to be accountable to the entire modern pentathlon community. Second, some activists claim that individuals in the UIPM leadership have a conflict of interest due to strong links to the sport of obstacle course racing. They also doubt whether individuals who occupy double roles in the IOC and the UIPM put the sport's interests first. The fact that the UIPM did not openly communicate potential conflict of interests, and individuals in leadership roles even attempted to delete connections to obstacle course racing, further aggravated the distrust by those affected by the UIPM's policies.

The UIPM will hold against the activists' arguments the need to modernize, the threat to lose a spot on the Olympic Games programme, and the installation of the 5th Discipline Commission to find a new sport. Importantly, Stull is not a member of that commission. Yet, considering how the power distribution has played out in the past within the UIPM, the activists find it easy to see how backroom deals have already been secured without their prior engagement.

In the overall dispute on accountability issues, the call of activists for participatory democracy shines through their arguments. They claim that the official elections do not give the modern pentathlon community sufficient power to judge over or influence the leadership. Thus, those in power can not only manipulate the elections but decide when to listen and when to ignore the voices from the community involved in modern pentathlon.

Transparency

According to the SGO, transparency refers to an organization's openness about internal working procedures, communication with all stakeholders and an honest exchange of information.[43] If applied successfully, transparency will ideally lead to enhanced trust amongst all involved interest groups as well as an understanding about the strategic plans of an organization.

Documentation

The activists argue that non-transparent procedures are used in an attempt to protect the current power structures and the leadership network. In short, transparency in an international sport federation context means that a governing body provides information so external audiences can monitor the procedures, decisions, and performances of the organization. The key here is, however, not to provide as much information as possible, but accurate information.[44] Some athletes suspect that the leadership assumes athletes are not interested in the federation's policies: "they think that we have no interest."

One cited example where the activists accuse the UIPM of lacking transparency, is the lack of willingness to publish minutes of meetings and make them available to the wider modern pentathlon community. Indeed, such alleged secrecy of the UIPM leadership can be seen in the lack of available meeting minutes from UIPM working group meetings. The UIPM has eight commissions and eight committees but the minutes of their meetings are only scarcely available on the UIPM website. The majority do not have any meeting minutes published online. Activist group members complained about this lack of transparency in the interviews. "It is not handy for the president to have minutes," one complained. "Everything is secret in the UIPM despite the fact that the president talks about transparency and democracy. But there is no value in it." As one important example, the UIPM's member federations have never seen the UIPM's Innovation Commission's minutes, even though this working group recommended - according to the UIPM's public communication - dropping horse-riding in the autumn of 2021.

Already in 2015, when the Governance Observer team evaluated the UIPM, the federation scored comparatively low in the transparency dimension.[45] Improvements were made and in a subsequent, though sport-internal, evaluation by ASOIF, the UIPM scored higher. However, as acknowledged by governance experts and as mentioned above, the scores do not reflect the reality of the practices within sport organizations. Statutes and general admissions to good governance principles are one thing, the consequent practical implementation of those principles another. From the perspective of the activists, the introduction of guidelines is not enough if they are not being followed in a stringent manner. Rather, the lack of transparency is considered the trigger that has led to speculation about the hidden rationales behind decisions.

According to one advocate, this could also be seen in the example of an earlier change in transparency rules. The interviewee reported that at a past Congress a NF put in a motion to allow for more transparent procedures. However, the majority of the UIPM leadership allegedly argued against the proposal. The Congress marginally voted to implement the changes and the UIPM later used the changes to publicly highlight its willingness to act in a transparent manner. Yet, the episode highlights that the degree of consent was very limited, and later statements in which the UIPM leadership congratulated itself for improvements in transparency might have to be challenged.

Without question, the accusations about the lack of transparent documentation must be considered as a consequence of the different interpretations of democratic principles. Whereas the UIPM leadership appears to act within the UIPM statutes, the activists demand much more transparency to allow for open debates and stakeholder engagement. For the activists, it is inevitable that at least key processes are open for public input and non-compliance with the transparency principle is a major hindrance for them in this regard.

Communication on the IOC's Role: A Pretextual Argument?

As outlined above, it cannot be denied that modern pentathlon is historically strongly tied to the Olympic Movement and the IOC. Until shortly after the Second World War, the IOC acted as the governing body of the sport and the two organizations share their founder in Pierre de Coubertin. In fact, many argue that modern pentathlon only remained continuously in the Olympic programme due to its special Olympic history. The UIPM leaders certainly used the historical ties when the IOC was on the verge of dropping the sport in the early 2000s, and have repeatedly maintained this argument ever since.[46]

Some activists brought up the significance of maintaining the historical disciplines in an attempt to secure modern pentathlon's place on the Olympic programme. "If you drop riding, then you make a new sport without historical ties and then essentially any five sports could be taken and that makes the UIPM so vulnerable." Indeed, the IOC lists one criteria for a sport to be included in the Olympic Games as "heritage and tradition."[47] It seems obvious that modern pentathlon received high scores in this category in previous evaluations due to the shared Coubertin link. Whether modern pentathlon can retain this high status once the UIPM has moved away from Coubertin's disciplines remains to be seen.

It is important to note, however, that the IOC is currently undergoing a major transition in various aspects.[48] First, the IOC attempts to connect with a younger audience - most notably through the invention of the Youth Olympic Games and the inclusion of action sports into the Olympic programme.[49] Second, it emphasizes the need for all Olympic stakeholders to modernize their governance and management structures, as seen in the example of the International Weightlifting Federation.[50] Third, as highlighted above, it increasingly recognizes athletes as politically active players within the Olympic Movement.[51] Those changes have also been notified by the activists and they acknowledge that modern pentathlon requires reform. However, they argue that the UIPM's reforms are not in the interest of the sport in the long-term, but merely serve only the interests of its leadership.

Against the background of the IOC's new-orientation, it is not surprising that the IOC argues that the UIPM must increase the youth appeal, accessibility, and safety of the sport. Certainly, an organization must constantly evolve and sport organizations have traditionally been slow to do so for the majority of their existence. The main issue here is not the fact that change is necessary, but *how* that change is being decided upon and implemented.

Many interviewed individuals argue that the UIPM misused the IOC in the communication on the horse-riding removal with statements that the IOC had coerced the UIPM into the decision. For example, the UIPM warned the modern pentathlon community - ahead of the congress' decision - that the IOC would only accept a proposal without riding when deciding over the future of the Olympic programme.[52] The activists reasoned that the IOC argument was pretextual and only used to justify the actions of the current leadership. One interviewee said: "The president had for more than a decade built up a narrative that he, and only he via his IOC connections, would be able to 'save' Modern Pentathlon's continued inclusion in the Olympic programme."

Some sources claim that putting forward the IOC demands is a pattern repeated in the UIPM leadership approach to criticism. For example, the UIPM informed members that the introduction of the 90-minutes programme was a direct response to the IOC requesting no sports programme to be longer than 90 minutes. Otherwise, the sports could not be fully broadcasted by the Olympic Broadcasting Services, the host broadcaster of all Olympic Games.[53]

The minutes of the 2021 UIPM Congress are equally unclear about the matter. At various points, the minutes mention that the UIPM leadership was told by the IOC to replace riding to achieve more global inclusivity. For example, it is noted: "In 2018, once more in our history, UIPM got a clear message from the IOC President. In a meeting with Dr. Thomas Bach, the IOC Sports Department, and the SG Shiny Fang a clear message was delivered that a solution to replace riding and make the sport more inclusive had to be made."[54] However, in other sections, the UIPM's legal counsel and IOC member Juan Antonio Samaranch highlighted that the IOC did not make a request to remove horse-riding.

The UIPM leadership further claims to have communicated with the IOC about the horse-riding removal, receiving its praise for the final decision. Following the decision at the 2021 UIPM congress, President Schormann informed the Congress participants on the next day that IOC President Thomas Bach and IOC Sports Director Kit McConnell had *congratulated* him personally on the decision. The congratulatory nature of the IOC messages was later reiterated by the UIPM's General Secretary.[55] It is of course impossible for the activists to verify the authenticity of such a message. Some member federations demanded that Schormann made available the IOC letters, but this was rejected.

Significantly, the IOC refers in official communication solely to a "UIPM decision,"[56] pushing all responsibility on to the federation. This was reiterated in the IOC's communication to put a decision about modern pentathlon's future in the Olympic programme on hold until 2023. On December 9, 2021, Thomas Bach explained in a press conference: "The UIPM must finalize *its proposal* for the replacement of horse riding and the overall competition format, and demonstrate a significant reduction in cost and complexity and an improvement across the areas of safety, accessibility, universality and appeal for young people and the general public (emphasis added)."[57] Such a stance appears reasonable as the Olympic Charter awards all rights and responsibilities to oversee sporting disciplines to the IFs.

The lack of transparency around the role of the IOC is further complicated through public statements by IOC members. Former IOC Vice-President Pal Schmitt wrote a letter to UIPM President Schormann, clearly stating that the UIPM claims of IOC pressure were wrong. The news outlet *Inside The Games*, which claims to have seen the letter, cited Schmitt as follows: "As an IOC member for 39 years, I can assure you that the IOC has never asked you to change the programme, the timing, the composition or the rules of modern pentathlon. (...) The IOC never asked you and your federation to drop horse riding from the programme."[58] Schmitt further explained that the IOC's host city contract with Los Angeles included modern pentathlon's traditional five disciplines. Athletes also recalled that during a meeting between the UIPM AC and IOC Sport Director McConnell in December 2021, he had highlighted that the IOC had not played an active role in the removal of horse-riding. Furthermore, McConnell argued that modern pentathlon's absence on the preliminary list of sports for the 2028 Olympic Games was not a reaction to the UIPM's decision. Finally, there is uncertainty about the role of Juan Antonio Samaranch, who serves as UIPM Vice-President and IOC member (and former IOC vice-president). As mentioned previously, the UIPM Executive Board unanimously voted in favor of finding a new discipline.

Disregard for Principles of Governance

In summary, though not directly linked to *internal* transparency procedures, the UIPM's unverified claims that the IOC pushed for the removal of horse-riding leaves the athlete community guessing about the real intentions behind the decision. This further reduced the trust of the athletes and the activist movement in the UIPM leadership. Coupled with an unwillingness to provide stakeholders with insights into minutes and working procedures, such lack of openness hindered the development of trust into the UIPM's strategies. However, irrespective of the UIPM's communication on the IOC role, it also emerged from the interviews that the athletes believed that only retaining horse-riding would ensure a inclusion of modern pentathlon on the Olympic programme in the long-term. One athlete stated: "the chances to stay in the Olympic Games in the long-term are lower if we ditch the connection to the sport's history." Many athletes highlighted the historical ties between modern pentathlon and Coubertin; one competitor reasoned that those links were a "guarantee" that the sport remained in the Olympic movement long-term. However, the competitor continued, "if we remove one of Coubertin's core sports, then a pentathlon could essentially consist of any five randomly put together disciplines."

Academia, non-governmental initiatives, and the institutional stakeholders within the international sport system agree in arguing that the correct rules and regulations within governing bodies of sport are a "prerequisite for obtaining good governance."[59] One must certainly agree with such a stance. There is good reason to believe that the UIPM has on paper followed recent reforms in sport and followed the implementation of such regulations. It was not the objective of this paper to investigate rules in place.

Rather, the contextualization of the accusations detailed in this chapter have demonstrated that the activists' viewpoints on the interpretation and employment of governance standards differs significantly from the UIPM leadership. They strongly promote progressive and liberal viewpoints and, on this basis, accuse the federation's leaders of various violations of good governance standards. The claim that the current leadership is not making open, democratic, and transparent decisions. In short, the activists accuse the UIPM leadership of misuse of power due to disregarding the voices of a large part of the modern pentathlon community, particularly the athletes. Indeed, this does not represent isolated allegations. Rather, the sum of the alleged wrongdoings give good reasons to suggest further investigations into the UIPM leadership. This becomes especially pertinent against the backdrop of other researchers' findings on mismanagement in sport organizations that were later confirmed by independent investigations. In short, the voices of the activists should no longer be ignored.

CONCLUSION

The Big Picture and Wider Implications

International sport is going through small but significant changes, much of which centers on addressing the ownership of sport. Influenced by public debates on freedom of speech, social movements such as Black Lives Matter, and human rights at mega-sport events such as the forthcoming 2022 FIFA World Cup in Qatar, some sports have begun to implement more athlete-centered policies. The impetus for such change in thinking has mainly come from the athletes' community itself. Athlete advocates, motivated by global movements towards equality, inclusion, and respect for human rights, have been successful in forcing sport to change, challenging who can exert power in sport organizations.

For example, the postponement of the 2020 Tokyo Olympic Games was, despite initial resistance from the IOC, driven by athletes and their concerns around health and safety issues in light of the Covid-19 pandemic.[1] The temporary amendment of the notorious Rule 50 of the Olympic Charter to allow athletes to protest at Olympic Games was a response to athletes' pressure, even though some critics consider the change only a public relations exercise.[2] In US gymnastics, athletes rather than the sport organizations drove the revelations against team doctor Larry Nassar, with high-profile competitors coming forward to expose his sexual abuse of hundreds of young girls. In Norway, female athletes successfully protested the bikini-bottom regulation that led to a change in their governing bodies' uniform policy. The list continues. Therefore, it certainly appears that many sports have arrived at the point at which the respective leadership has to make a decision on whether it wants to continue exploiting athletes or whether it wants to engage with them on equal terms. Some sports have made a step into the direction of a 50-50 relationship with athletes, often forced to do so by public pressure or a crisis in governance. An equal relationship in decision-making is only one alternative model of sport governance with more athletes' representation, however. Attributing athletes with veto rights is another option that is currently debated. Come what may, athletes have challenged the ownership of sport.

The athletes movement in modern pentathlon is yet another powerful example of this unfolding trend. The thesis presented in this book is that by focusing more closely on athlete advocates opinions and viewpoints, they can provide important leverage to the top-down processes within the sport system. The athletes' advocate group analyzed in this study reported that the UIPM has a strong disregard for the voices of athletes and accused the federation of abuse as regards the principles of good governance. The interviewed athletes argue that the UIPM is caught up in problematic organizational cultures, controlled by its current leadership. The activists claim that the UIPM leadership acts according to self-interest and has willingly ignored severe issues with the horse-riding discipline. The UIPM did not attempt to solve the challenge with equestrianism, but opted to drop the discipline altogether. By doing so, the athletes' advocates argue, the UIPM leadership's power abuse became so apparent that their actions could no longer be ignored.

The activists can be considered a social movement in the sense that they demand rights and recognition for a group - the participating athletes - that is excluded from participation in the decision-making even though they are an essential part of the modern pentathlon community. After all, the athletes are the one group most impacted by any rules and decisions taken by the governing body. Jasper highlights that human action is full of different viewpoints, but "only rarely and temporarily are large groups able to speak with one voice, as they do in social movements."[3] This certainly reflects the case study in question. The activists opposing the current UIPM leadership are not random opportunists, mere protesters or even rebels. They must be regarded as athletes' advocates, aiming to expose the mismanagement in modern pentathlon. When UIPM President Klaus Schormann is quoted in an UIPM press release about the inaugural meeting of the 5th Discipline Working Group saying: "to have such a *collective determination from our athletes* in this vital endeavor is hugely important (emphasis added),"[4] he seems to portray an entirely different picture about the athletes' standpoints. This study indicates that many athletes *oppose* the UIPM's decision. The UIPM appears to have therefore very little - if any - backing from within the group of *independent* athletes.

The activists put forward progressive and liberal understandings of governance. The rights of the individual athletes participating in modern pentathlon and the threat posed by the UIPM leadership to those rights form the focal point for their arguments. Their calls for an end of the athletes' marginalization are aligned with a strong belief in the positive effects of stakeholder participation. Their accusations of non-transparent decision-making, power abuse, and lack of accountability build on such an understanding. They argue that the current interpretation and - in some cases - ignorance of the democratic principles as set out in the UIPM statutes severely undermine the legitimacy of the decisions made by the UIPM leadership.

Readers are reminded that the purpose of this book was not to evaluate those UIPM rules and regulations. Rather, it explores accusations on how its leadership interprets (or decides to circumvent) the rulebook. The charges are serious: ranging from non-transparent communication over individual conflict of interests to allegations of clientelism. The latter allegation is a particularly severe one. The activist group argues that the current UIPM leadership is nigh on impossible to shift with the current power balances in place because it accumulated a concentration of power based on the dependencies of small NFs. Some of these do not even engage in the sport. As a result, the current leadership can easily abuse its power.

For the large majority of the interviewees, the removal of the riding discipline was the last, and most severe, action of power abuse by the UIPM leadership, triggered by its failure to engage in an open and honest communication within the athlete community about this decision. The athletes identified that the UIPM's line of actions was not an exception either. Strong claims were made that the introduction of the 90-minute format was a precursor of things to come. Coupled with the marginalization of athletes, such accusations puts the movement in a very strong position vis-a-vis the current leadership. Independent investigations into the claims appear inevitable.

A significant finding is the level of engagement of high-level athletes in the protests and their interest in the politics at play in the sport of pentathlon. Commentators often correctly excuse athletes for not having the time and capacity to become involved in decision-making processes within their sports. Indeed, even some of the former athletes questioned for this study claimed that former competitors had to step in for athletes who are still active. However, this was not the case here. The elite athletes in modern pentathlon are very engaged in political debates, even though

Conclusion: The Big Picture and Wider Implications

they effectively continue to be ignored by the UIPM leadership. Thus, their expertise and interest in governance issues provided here refutes often made claims that athletes lack the necessary knowledge to get involved with sporting political processes. More athletes, also from other sports, could take the modern pentathletes as examples. The current trend certainly points towards an increasing number of athletes showing their potential power in solidarity with fellow competitors.

The removal of horse-riding has brought the modern pentathlon community together and the percentage of athletes opposing the UIPM is extraordinarily high. It is obvious that the relatively low popularity of the sport, its lack of media attention, and the absence of superstars complicates the athletes' position in modern pentathlon. It is difficult to see how World Athletics would in the current sport political climate ignore the voices of past and present superstars. Just imagine Usain Bolt, Allyson Felix, and Jessica Holmes joining forces to protest a severe change in the sport of track and field. However, it appears that just like the UIPM seems to utilize the sport's low profile to establish an uncontestable power base, the small sporting community can turn into an advantage for the activists. "If you have no athletes, if you have no coaches, you have no sport," one athlete summarized a possible scenario for the UIPM. Thus, if the modern pentathlon community of athletes, coaches, and some NFs join forces, they might create a momentum that brings the current developments to a halt.

At the very least, and here parallels to other sports such as swimming or athletics are inevitable, there is a possibility to create an independent athletes' body through which the athletes can speak with a collective voice in dialogue with the UIPM. The athletes need to know that there are competing values on equality and participation, however, and the argument driven forward here is only one way to view the situation. The governing bodies of sport historically have little interest in giving away degrees of power to their stakeholders. Moreover, other commentators, scholars, and particularly sport administrators might be able to demonstrate that the UIPM leadership acts within a perfectly justifiable democratic framework. Others might say, some corrections need to be made and selected violations of democratic principles addressed, but generally the governance system in the federation is adequate.

With negotiations between the two opponents likely to be difficult (if not impossible), the activists' success depends to a large degree on their legitimation of their, on first view, traditionalist views on the future of the sport and their opposition towards calls for removal of riding due to animal welfare issues. It is clear that the activists have progressive, participatory, and liberal viewpoints on the governance of sport. Therefore it might be irritating for some attentive observers that they appear to foster tradition, heritage, and strong opposition to changes in their sport, which speaks directly to modern pentathlon's critics. However, it is vital to note that all activists genuinely care for animal safety. None of the interviewed individuals downplayed the welfare of the horses. On the contrary, the activists have convincingly argued that they, more than anyone else involved in modern pentathlon, care for the horses, and have numerous reform ideas to significantly improve the riding discipline. What is more, they claimed that the UIPM leadership ignored the horse-riding issue for decades and now uses recent scandals as an excuse for large-scale reform of the sport.

Whether the activists can provide significant alternatives to the current governance of the sport thus depends on its ability to marshal their protests into feasible reform suggestions and to demonstrate to potential allies that they are indeed progressive and deeply committed to the future of the sport. This study contributes to this quest. If the athletes are able to present realistic suggestions for reform, the IOC appears to be in a very difficult position to ignore the activists' calls. The movement itself speaks directly to the ongoing trend in the Olympic Movement to rhetorically subordinate all strategies to the principle of "putting athletes first." Consequently, if the IOC actually commits to the changes that the organization promotes, it must pay attention to the issues raised by the athletes over the course of this research project.

Moreover, it appears to be important to demonstrate publicly the common ground within the large majority of the modern pentathlon community and work together towards their goals. The athletes must take the lead in this process, and if some of the movement's leaders divert from the jointly decided pathway, they must be called out. If the individuals within the movement can proceed jointly, then there is a possibility to resist potential domination of individual voices. It is evident that the distrust prevalent within the athletes' community does not allow for the continued hiding of the UIPM leadership. In many other sport organizations, leaders have failed to listen to their athletes' communities and were accused of power abuse in the not too distant past. Lamine Diack, Joseph Blatter, Tamas Ajan, the list continues. They all failed to step out, others did and failed in desperate attempts to maintain power. Eventually, they all faced public investigations and were forced to leave international sport with negative reputations (and in some cases court convictions!). It appears that the current UIPM leadership has also arrived at this crossroad, and the more "united" Pentathlon United will be, the more likely the movement is to decide which turn the UIPM leadership will take.

The gain in knowledge through this research was only possible through the athlete-centered approach. Switching the focus to those affected by a sport organization's policies allowed for the exploration of the perceived reality behind the facade of good governance principles and regulations. This research provides evidence for the assumption that in order to disclose hidden realities, it is important to investigate beneath the surface and rhetoric of international sport.[5] Whilst such an approach is often associated with critical journalism to generate income and attention, this study takes a different pathway. It provides context, interpretation, and an assessment of the athletes' perspectives. Obviously, by taking the described point of departure for this study, an assumption is made that the power balance in sport is not equal. This is the nature of the critical social research framework adopted here. But the researcher does not go as far as to engage himself in the activism as an activist per se. If the athletes utilize the knowledge produced here the situation is now in their own hands.

In spite of the uniqueness of this study, and as a result of it, this study has limitations that need to be addressed. I stated at the outset in this book that it is impossible to set aside personal values and retain *complete* objectivity in qualitative research.[6] Thus, the UIPM leadership might argue that the approach taken here does not present a balanced account of the ongoing issue because they were not directly asked about their opinion as regards the framework for this research. In fact, such skepticism by authorities towards the exposure of dominant power relations is to be expected.[7] However, this was never the objective of this research. The response to the reviewers in this book directly answers such criticism. Instead, it was always the intention from the beginning to focus on the viewpoints of the disempowered: to produce knowledge, contextualize their movement, and evaluate the statements of peers. The study thereby complements the athletes' surveys and petitions which demonstrate the numerical evidence for the athletes' opposition to positions adopted by the UIPM. This does not mean that the UIPM's viewpoints were entirely absent from this study. On the contrary, they are strongly considered in the text through public statements, communication with the athletes, and internal documents. And whilst the UIPM leadership does not take center stage in this book, it remains in control of all processes, and as the stakeholder in power it will have multiple avenues open to answer the accusations emanating from the community of athletes.

Today, modern pentathlon faces a unique moment in its history; not merely because horse-riding has been removed from the sport. Rather, the ongoing developments are a window of opportunity to fight for real, lasting change. The athletes' movement is aligned with current wider political trends to fight for more inclusion, equality, and participation globally. The activists clearly promote progressive values and have concrete ideas for reforms of their sport - on and off the field. The athletes might not have come on horses to deliver their messages, but their communications are clear: changes are necessary to save the sport of modern pentathlon. The athletes have pressed their charges.

AFTERWORD

Response to Reviewers

The peer-review process is today the most important and preferred method to check the validity of academic works. Ideally, peer-reviews aim to examine texts and studies for their *independent* value. As a result, peer-review appears to be the guarantee of quality for academic work. We, as editors of the *Sharp Ideas* book series, argue however, that the peer-review process as a means to assess the contents of publications is over-exaggerated. Peer-reviews can help to improve the quality of manuscripts, check the consistency of arguments, and serve as a valuable tool to verify facts and information. Yet, we believe that the peer-review process should not, as it is the case in many academic journals and books series, a form of paternalism and censorship because manuscripts must be significantly altered to the views of the reviewers (or editors) before they are accepted.

Our views appear to be in line with the original intentions behind the implementation of the process. These were not aimed toward verification and quality assurance. As philosopher Susan Haack notes, pre-publication peer review was invented only as an initial screening process to filter academic work. Based on such historical considerations, she further argues that today's interpretation of the process as an indication of quality is exaggerated.[1] Similarly, the former editor of the *British Medical Journal*, Richard Smith, formulated a strong assessment of the peer-review process when arguing: "Peer review is slow, expensive, profligate of academic time, highly subjective, prone to bias, easily abused, poor at detecting gross defects, and almost useless in detecting fraud."[2] In 2006, Smith was asked to published a volume of the *British Medical Journal* that included only papers rejected by peer-review. He answered: "How do you know I haven't already done it?".[3]

In the humanities and social sciences, the core academic fields of the books published in this series, research results are difficult to be falsified and objectively evaluated. This is particularly the case when the books address aspects from different research areas such as history, sociology, political science, and philosophy. Historians might want authors to focus on different issues than philosophical scientists. Similarly, political views and ideologies might influence the reviewers' verdicts. Michael J. Mahony raised such concerns already in 1977, when he claimed that reviewers tend to positively evaluate publications that confirm their own views, as opposed to those that do not.[4]

Therefore, rather than letting reviewers decide on what will be published in this book series and potentially strangle the life out of sharp ideas before they can be spread, we provide authors with the possibility to respond to reviews directly. To be sure, we still value the peer-review process as an important tool to "pre-screen" publications, in line with the original intentions. However, we believe that there must be a room to reject reviews based on solid argumentation. Based on those pre-considerations, I will respond to the reviewers of my manuscript in the following section.

In the case of *Athletes Pressing Charges*, the two reviewers commended the initial manuscript and mainly provided smaller suggestions for improvement. I have made changes to the text according to their recommendations. I would like to thank both reviewers for engaging in detail with my text in a short period of time and helping me to improve the manuscript. Their positive response to my text makes it a tricky task to respond and "defend" the arguments I raised in the book. After all, they generally agree with my viewpoints and the significance of the study. That said, one reviewer, to whom I will refer to as R2 because it was the second review I received, raised one major concern that I would like to address on the following pages in detail. R2 criticizes my approach of not directly engaging with the UIPM's leadership in my study in several paragraphs of the review. For example, R2 writes:

> *I would argue that good social science should take into account the position of all (or most) of the sub-groups or organisational stakeholders. If not, there a risk that what appears to be radical, and therefore good critical social science which supports marginalised groups, is in fact weakened by imbalance and bias.*

The statement echoes perceptions of the academic community who argue that scientific research is only legitimate and valid when it is "completely" objective. I contest that viewpoint and will argue in this response to R2 that my approach can be justified because it adds diversity to the discussion on athletes' representation in decision-making. Rather than explaining my perspective based on existing academic literature as I do in the main text, I attempt to speak directly to the reviewer and provide personal viewpoints.

First, I argued in the text that when we conduct research, design our studies, and write up the results, we always make decisions on how our research is put forward. The perspectives, values, social experiences, and viewpoints of the researcher always influence our work. I understand that this can make it difficult for readers to assess our work as scientific and independent. However, I adopt here a critical paradigm where subjectivity is a reality and objectivity in social research rejected. As social scientists, we should admit that our conclusions are always influenced by our internal advocacies because we make judgements based on our human experiences. In fact, I believe the practice of reflexivity has become a necessary step in methodological inquiry; the researcher should always incorporate how perspectives are temporarily embedded for themselves and their participants. So, if we as researchers have a more sympathetic attitude towards activists, as I unquestionably had in this book, we should not deny such views as not academic but rather promote their arguments to improve situations and systems. When taking such a standpoint that dismisses the existence of value-free research, it is important to be transparent about value judgements so policy makers can better assess how they should digest the provided information and scientific claims.[5]

Second, it appears virtually impossible to give all stakeholders and especially all "*individuals who hold positions of management or leadership*" a voice as R2 demands. We do have to decide on what our main research interests are and this decision is influenced by the general considerations I raised in the previous paragraph. Feminist researchers, for example, have long promoted the view that objectivity is an impossibility and idealization of the research process. They argue that women's views have been ignored for centuries in what men claim to be "objective" research.[6]

I prefer to refer to work within my original field of research, sport history, to elaborate further, however. For decades, large junks of sport history have been written based on the documentation collected by sport organizations and press reports with very little consideration for the participating athletes. Those works are widely celebrated, and I do not think anyone can make a claim that those histories are severely weakened because they did not engage with other stakeholders, particularly the athletes. Let us only focus on the history of doping, for example. Paul Dimeo has written an excellent and incredibly well-researched account of the early history of performance-enhancing drugs, showing drug use in sport has a long history that dates to the end of the nineteenth century.[7] Dimeo could not have interviewed many athletes from that time and there are few notes available from participants illustrating their drug use. Does this make it a weak account of the history of doping in sport because not all stakeholders are considered equally? I do not think so. Similarly, Thomas Hunt has written a brilliant institutional history of the IOC's anti-doping fight, largely based on archival sources collected from the IOC's archives.[8] We do not find a lot of engagement with athletes' viewpoints in his book but that does not make it a weak text. My colleague (and co-editor of this book series) Verner Møller takes an entirely different approach when he studies in-depth the case of Danish cyclist Michael Rasmussen and uses his story to criticize the anti-doping system.[9] Møller highlights in his preface that he mainly relied on Rasmussen's material and interviewed the cyclist many times but argues that he does not present a one-sided view because he included all available information in the analysis. Yet, he argues that he was mainly interested in the works that did not make it into the public sphere. Møller's book adds another perspective to the understanding of the complex field of anti-doping, even though he did not equally consider the views from all sides.

My point with presenting those examples from doping history research is that my approach that focuses on the athletes' voices is that it adds diversity to the understanding of athletes' representation in global sport in general and the controversy in modern pentathlon specifically. R2 asks, "*should we, as social scientists, be encouraging one section of a community to 'drive the narrative'?*" I believe we can because it exposes readers to different views, particularly when the community has not been heard before. Black scholars, for example, alerted us that about a reality that a focus on actors already in power allows their own narrative control to be reproduced and continuously silence more marginalized voices.[10] The impetus for this research is to add to a larger body of knowledge on how athletes are being ignored and exploited in decision-making processes within international sport. There is a lack of awareness, both, in the public as well as in academia, about athletes' viewpoints and especially their attempts in advocating for a greater say in decisions that directly affect their sporting careers. Therefore, I consciously provide them with the room to make their voices heard and analyze their statements to contribute to my goal of creating better circumstances for athletes around the world – whether that is in modern pentathlon or other sports. I feel empowered to pursue that goal in this way.

I do not suggest that the activists or marginalized groups perspectives are superior to those by the powerful. I just suggest that they are different and have the potential to improve the overall situation of governance in global sport. I hold it with Ben Jones, who recently discussed the proper relationship between research and politics. He argues that without working closely with activists – or researchers even becoming themselves activists – "research likely would suffer from certain blind spots and overlook aspects of politics that those directly involved in such work would be more likely to notice."[11] Thus, by adopting a specific, activist viewpoint, researchers can produce knowledge that would not materialize if the research remained outside the research process. And as I have shown throughout the book, I believe that the athletes in modern pentathlon do see their involvement and their understanding of the governance of their sport very differently than how research and public accounts portray them. In my view, this return to people's point of views and their ends of action, is a sharp perspective within the discussion of governance of sport. As members of the public and researchers we are often only given those perspectives of those in leadership - far less often do we have access to the athletes' perspectives. I am driving forward the idea that by listening to the athletes, those who are mostly affected by sport organizations' policies, we can point out mismanagement and hopefully improve sport governance in the long-term. Athletes are not passive observers, especially not when such significant issues are at stake that change an entire sport.

Finally, as I do highlight in the text, the UIPM's view is represented in the text and the athletes' statement contrasted with the publicly available statements from the UIPM leadership. In fact, whilst the first draft of this manuscript was in revision, I was able to gather more documentation such as congress minutes and the UIPM's justification within the UIPM's Court of Arbitration case. It is not necessary to collect the same data (i.e. interviews) or use the same method for every piece of the argument, especially if there is no gain for the research itself. I agree with C. Wright Mills, who argued that we should not waste our time designing studies or conduct interviews when we can find the answers in books in libraries.[12] Similarly, when the UIPM leaders have justified their viewpoints in television interviews, official statements, and press reports, why would they give away more details in an academic interview setting? Many of the main individuals within the UIPM leadership have been in an executive position for several decades. They had forums and possibilities to raise their voices for decades and I strongly doubt that they would have provided me with, as R2 suggest, *justifications that were made to side-line athletes' perspectives and exclude athletes from governance processes*. After all, the UIPM publicly claims that the athletes were not excluded from the policy processes at all.

This not to say that the athletes' statements were not subject to a thorough analysis. I told many of the gatekeepers and athletes I interviewed for this study that they should not expect a one-sided presentation, but a discussion of their arguments. They agreed with this position as they realized that any reader of the book must be provided with sufficient information to make own judgements of the situations. I believe that I have done this even without, as R2 suggests, to directly approach the UIPM. Thus, just like Verner Møller in *The Scapegoat*, I adopt a perspective that focuses on athletes affected by policies - crucially - without ignoring the policy-makers viewpoints.

NOTES

Preface

1. Ian McDonald, "Critical social research and political intervention: moralistic versus radical approaches," in *Power games: A Critical Sociology of Sport*, ed. John Sugden and AlanTomlinson (Abingdon/New York: Routledge, 2002), 100-116.
2. Arnout Geerært and Frank von Eerkeren, *Good Governance in Sport. Critical Reflections* (Abingdon/New York: Routledge, 2021), xii.

Introduction

1. "Joe Choong: Olympic modern pentathlon champion fears changes could end sport," *BBC*, November 10, 2021, https://www.bbc.com/sport/olympics/59232363.
2. Jean-Loup Chappelet, "The unstoppable rise of athlete power in the Olympic system," *Sport in Society* 23, no. 5 (2020): 795-809. https://doi.org/10.1080/17430437.2020.17 48817. Also see: Helen Lenskyj, The Olympic Games. A Critical Approach (Bingley: Emerald, 2020).
3. Yetsa A. Tuakli-Wosornu, Demetri Goutos, Ioana Ramia, Natalie R. Galea, Margo Mountjoy, Katharina Grimm, and Sheree Bekker, "Development and validation of the athletes' rights survey," *BMJ Open Sport & Exercise Medicine* 7, no. 4 (2021): 1-10. https://doi.org/10.1136/bmjsem-2021-001186.
4. See for example the 2019 Sports Governance Observer here: https://www.playthegame.org/knowledge-bank/downloads/sports-governance-observer-2019/275a52c3-c8a0-4a85-8b8f-aae2008a03c1.
5. John Sugden and Alan Tomlinson, "Digging the Dirt and Staying Clean: Retrieving the Investigative Tradition for a Critical Sociology of Sport," *International Review for the Sociology of Sport* 34, no. 4 (1999): 385-397. https://doi.org/10.1177/101269099034004006.
6. See for example Richard McLaren's independent investigation on corruption in the International Weightlifting Federation (IWF) here: https://www.mclarenglobalsportsolutions.com/pdf/FinalReport_IWF_June6_2020.pdf.

The Approach

1. There is also no legal foundation to justify any of the IOC's powers, see Alexandre Mestre, "The legal basis of the Olympic Charter," *The International Sports Law Journal* no. 1-2 (2007).
2. "Olympic Charter," *International Olympic Committee*, accessed January 17, 2022. https://stillmed.olympic.org/media/Document%20Library/OlympicOrg/General/EN-Olympic-Charter.pdf.
3. Andrea Cattaneo and Richard Parrish, *Sports Law and Policy in the European Union*

(Manchester: Manchester University Press, 2003).
4. John J. MacAloon, "Scandal and governance: inside and outside the IOC 2000 Commission," *Sport in Society* 14, no. 3 (2001): 292-308, https://doi.org/10.1080/17430437.2011.557265.
5. Margareta Baddeley, "The Extraordinary Autonomy of Sports Bodies under Swiss Law: Lessons to be Drawn," *The International Sports Law Journal* 20 (2020): 3-17, https://doi.org/10.1007/s40318-019-00163-6.
6. Peter Donnelly, "What if the players controlled the game? Dealing with the consequences of the crisis of governance in sports," *European Journal for Sport and Society* 12, no. 1 (2015): 11-30. https://doi.org/10.1080/16138171.2015.11687954.
7. Brendan Schwab, "'Celebrating Humanity': Reconciling Sport and Human Rights Through Athlete Activism," *Journal of Legal Aspects of Sport* 28, no. 1-2 (2018): 170-207.
8. Brendan Schwab, "Embedding the human rights of players in world sport," *The International Sports Law Journal* 17 (2018): 214-232, https://link.springer.com/article/10.1007/s40318-018-0128-9.
9. Daniela Heerdt, *Blurred lines of responsibility and accountability: Human rights abuses at mega-sporting events* (Cambridge: Intersentia, 2021).
10. Cattaneo and Parrish, *Sports Law*.
11. Maximilian Seltmann, "Disrupting institutional reproduction? How Olympic athletes challenge the stability of the Olympic Movement," *Sport und Gesellschaft* 18, no. 1 (2021): 9-37, https://doi.org/10.1515/sug-2021-0002.
12. Hannah Borenstein, "On Your Mark, Get Set, Unionise," *Tribune*, August 22, 2020, https://tribunemag.co.uk/2020/08/on-your-marks-get-set-unionise.
13. Maximilian Seltmann, "Disrupting institutional reproduction?."
14. Jules Boykoff, "Protest, Activism, and the Olympic Games: An Overview of Key Issues and Iconic Moments," *International Journal of the History of Sport* 34, no. 3-4 (2017), 162-183. https://doi.org/10.1080/09523367.2017.1356822.
15. BR24 Wintersport (@BR24Wintersport), "'Warum müssen wir in ein Land gehen, das keinen Bezug zum Wintersport hat? DSV-Alpindirektor Wolfgang Maiers Vorfreude auf Olympia in Peking hält sich in Grenzen. Das Interview ist Teil der BR / ARD Doku 'Spiel mit dem Feuer' mit @felix_neureuther. Die gibt's bereits jetzt in der ARD Mediathek und am 31.01. um 20:15 Uhr in der ARD. #BR24Wintersport #Olympia #Peking #Maier #felixneureuther #nosnownoshow #olympischespiele," *Instagram*, January 29, 2021, https://www.instagram.com/p/CZTzcdjqosj/?utm_medium=share_sheet.
16. Ibid.
17. Stephan Wassong, *The International Olympic Committee Athletes' Commission: Its Foundation, Development & Transition*, 1981-2000 (Cologne: German Sport University, 2021).
18. Lucie Thibault, Lisa Kihl and Kathy Babiak, "Democrati-zation and Governance in International Sport: Addressing Issues with Athlete Involvement in Organizational Policy," *International Journal of Sport Policy and Politics* 2, no. 3 (2010): 275–302, https://doi.org/10.1080/19406940.2010.507211.
19. "UIPM Constitutional Book," *UIPM World Pentathlon*.
20. Seltmann, "Disrupting institutional reproduction?."
21. "Code of Ethics," *Fédération Internationale de Natation*, accessed February 3, 2022, https://resources.fina.org/fina/document/2021/01/12/c9057283-1c4e-442e-807e-f88c982c7275/logo_fina_code_of_ethics_as_approved_by_the_ec_on_22.07.2017_final_0.pdf.
22. Seltmann, "Disrupting institutional reproduction?," 17.
23. Mike Rowbottom, "Exclusive: Olympian Wickenheiser reveals how she was criticised by IOC over comments calling for Tokyo 2020 postponement," *insidethegames*, April 12, 2020, https://www.insidethegames.biz/articles/1093067/hayley-wickenheis-

er-ppe-opc-canada.
24. Helen Lenskyj, *The Olympic Games. A Critical Approach* (Bingley: Emerald, 2020), 110.
25. Helen Lenskyj, "Let the Games Begin? The Decision to Postpone the Tokyo 2020 Summer Olympics," in *Time Out. Global Perspectives on Sport and the Covid-19 Lockdown*, ed. Jörg Krieger, April Henning, Lindsay Pieper, and Paul Dimeo (Champaign: Commonground, 2021), 15-28.
26. See for example the EMPLOYS project at the German Sport University Cologne: https://www.dshs-koeln.de/institut-fuer-europaeische-sportentwicklung-und-freizeitforschung-jean-monnet-lehrstuhl/forschung-projekte/laufende-projekte/employs-understanding-evaluating-and-improving-good-governance/.
27. Stephan Wassong, Angela J. Schneider, and Rob Hess, "The Voice of the Athlete in History: An Overview," *The International Journal of the History of Sport* 38, no. 10-11 (2021), 1029-1034, https://doi.org/10.1080/09523367.2021.1995360.
28. Donnelly, "What if the players controlled the game?."
29. Maximilian Seltmann, "The Institutional Position of Athletes in the Governance Networks of the Olympic Movement in Canada, Germany and the United Kingdom," *The International Journal of the History of Sport* 38, no. 10-11 (2021): 1165-1188, https://doi.org/10.1080/09523367.2021.1978428.
30. Lenskyj, *The Olympic Games*, 119.
31. Belinda Wheaton, "Babes on the beach, women in the surf: researching gender, power and difference in the windsurfing culture," in *Power games: A Critical Sociology of Sport*, ed. John Sugden and Alan Tomlinson (Abingdon/New York: Routledge, 2002), 240-266.
32. Richard G. Fox, ed., *Recapturing Anthropology. Working in the Present* (Santa Fe: School of American Research Press, 1992).
33. "Ensuring Access to Effective Remedy," *World Players Association*, accessed February 1, 2022, https://uniglobalunion.org/sites/default/files/files/news/wpa_access_to_remedy_0.pdf.
34. Carbonella, August, and Sharryn Kasmir, "Dispossession, Disorganization and The Anthropology of Labor," in *Anthropologies of Class. Power, Practice, and Inequality*, ed. James G. Carrier and Don Kalb (Cambridge: Cambridge University Press, 2015), 41-52. Susanna Narotzky, "Structures without Soul and Immediate Struggles: Rethinking Militant Particularism in Contemporary Spain," in *Blood and Fire: Toward a Global Anthropology of Labor*, ed. Sharryn Kasmir and August Carbonella (New York: Berghan Book, 2014), 167–203.
35. Ian McDonald, "Critical social research," 101.
36. Ibid., 108.
37. Charles R. Hale, "What is activist research?," *Items* 2, no. 1–2 (2001), 13–15.
38. James M. Jasper, *The Art of Moral Protest: Culture, Biography, and Creativity in Social Movements* (Chicago: University of Chicago Press, 1998).
39. James M. Jasper, *The Emotions of Protest* (Chicago: University of Chicago Press, 2018).
40. James M. Jasper, "Cultural Approaches in the Sociology of Social Movements," in *Handbook of Social Movements Across Disciplines*, ed. Bert Klandermans and Conny Roggeband (New York: Springer, 2010), 59-109.
41. Three interviews were conducted with a translator.
42. Letter, Russian Modern Pentathlon Federation Athletes' Committee to UIPM Athletes' Committee, 26 November 2021.
43. James M. Jasper, *Protest: A Cultural Introduction to Social Movements* (Cambridge: Polity Press, 2014).

Modern Pentathlon

1. See for example announcement of media experts to working group: "UIPM Welcomes Four Media and Marketing Experts to 5th Discipline Working Group," *UIPM World Pentathlon*, December 22, 2021, https://www.uipmworld.org/news/uipm-welcomes-four-media-and-marketing-experts-5th-discipline-working-group?fbclid=IwAR05jZbQw9Ct9r-FjRd07PUfgg1AaN8Lr62nSH6pqe4gZejI6Ch41xjzvII.
2. The disciplines also marked a departure from the ancient pentathlon, which consisted of a foot race, wrestling, long jump, javelin, and discus throw.
3. Unknown author, "The Origins of the Modern Pentathlon," in *Olympism. Selected Writings*, ed. Norbert Müller (Lausanne: International Olympic Committee, 2000): 445-446. Readers should note that the original text is unsigned but was by the editor, Norbert Müller, determined to be from Pierre de Coubertin.
4. Pierre de Coubertin, "Budapest (1911)," in *Olympism. Selected Writings*, ed. Norbert Müller (Lausanne: International Olympic Committee, 2000): 433.
5. Ansgar Molzberger, "Die Olympischen Spiele 1912 in Stockholm - 'Vaterländische' Spiele als Durchbruch für die Olympische Bewegung" (PhD. diss., German Sport University Cologne, 2010), 104.
6. Patrick Clastres, "Performance sportive et prouesse olympique selon Pierre de Coubertin," *Les Cahiers de l'INSEP*, no. 46 (2010), 193-202. https://doi.org/10.3406/insep.2010.1128.
7. Sandra Heck, "William Penny Brookes - the Founding Father of the Modern Pentathlon?," *Sport in History* 34, no. 1: 75-89. https://doi.org/10.1080/17460263.2013.873074.
8. Sandra Heck, "A Sport for Everyone? Inclusion and Exclusion in the Organization of the First Olympic Modern Pentathlon," *The International Journal of the History of Sport* 31, no. 5 (2014): 526-541. https://doi.org/10.1080/09523367.2013.798305.
9. Ibid.
10. Molzberger, "Die Olympischen Spiele 1912 in Stockholm," 122.
11. Sandra Heck, "Modern Pentathlon and the First World War: When athletes and Soldiers Met to Practise Martial Manliness," *The International Journal of the History of Sport* 28, no. 3-4 (2011): 410-428. https://doi.org/.10.1080/09523367.2011.544860.
12. Sandra Heck, "Modern Pentathlon and the First World War: When Athletes and Soldiers Met to Practise Martial Manliness," in *Sport, Militarism and the Great War: Martial Manliness and Armageddon*, eds. Thierry Terret and J.A. Mangan (Abingdon/New York: Routledge, 2012), 89-107.
13. Sandra Heck, "Modern Pentathlon at the 2012 London Olympics: Between Traditional Heritage and Modern Changes for Survival," *The International Journal of the History of Sport* 30, no. 7 (2013): 719-735. https://doi.org/10.1080/09523367.2013.782485.
14. Ibid.
15. "Special Edition: Refuting IOC's Plan to End Modern Pentathlon Competition," *The Sport Journal*, https://web.archive.org/web/20120605032621/http://thesportjournal.org/article/special-edition-sport-journal-ioc-planning-drop-modern-pentathlon-olympic-games.

  Ian Ritchie, "Pierre de Coubertin, Doped 'Amateurs' and the 'Spirit of Sport': The Role of Mythology in Olympic Anti-Doping Policies," *The International Journal of the History of Sport* 31, no. 8 (2014): 820-838, https://doi.org/10.1080/09523367.2014.883500.
16. Heck, "Modern Pentathlon at the 2012 London Olympics."
17. James Toney, "Modern Pentathlon: A sport in danger of being consigned to Olympic history by old indecision and new influence," *The Independent*, August 5, 2021, https://

www.independent.co.uk/sport/olympics/modern-pentathlon-choong-french-tokyo-2020-b1897407.html.
18. "Vision, Mission, Values, and Strategic Plan," *UIPM World Pentathlon*, accessed January 27, 2022, https://www.uipmworld.org/vision-mission-values-and-strategic-plan.
19. Molzberger, "Die Olympischen Spiele 1912 in Stockholm," 118n104.
20. Bonnie Berkowitz and Artur Galocha, "Who dominated the Olympics? Depends on the sport," *The Washington Post*, July 21, 2021, https://www.washingtonpost.com/sports/olympics/2021/07/21/olympic-sport-dominance-country/.
21. This includes athletes from the former German Democratic Republic.
22. Molzberger, "Die Olympischen Spiele 1912 in Stockholm," 124.
23. David Campbell, "Pentathlon is one, big unappealing mess," *Cleveland*, March 28, 2019, https://www.cleveland.com/olympics/2008/08/penthathon_is_one_big_unappeal.html.
24. Mike Rowbottom, "New modern pentathlon format for Paris 2024 gets thumbs up at final test event," *insidethegames*, April 27, 2021, https://www.insidethegames.biz/articles/1107148/uipm-paris-2024-format-test-event.
25. Stephanie Heinicke, "Medialisierung im Spitzensport: Eine Erfolgsgeschichte?," *Journal für Sportkommunikation und Mediensport* 1, no. 1-2 (2016): 42-52, https://doi.org/10.25968/JSkMs.2016.1-2.42-52
26. Heck, "Modern Pentathlon at the 2012 London Olympics."
27. Mike Canter, "Every Single Olympic Event Ranked: 339-251," *Slate*, July 22, 2021, https://slate.com/culture/2021/07/tokyo-olympics-worst-sports-events-ranking.html.
28. Heck, "Modern Pentathlon at the 2012 London Olympics."
29. Pete Nichols, "Olympics: Horse farce dominates modern pentathlon," *The Guardian*, August 21, 2008, https://www.theguardian.com/sport/2008/aug/21/olympics2008.olympicsmodernpentathlon.
30. Flora Watkins, "Is the standard of pentathlon jumping up to scratch?," *Horse and Hound*, August 23, 2012, https://www.horseandhound.co.uk/news/is-the-standard-of-pentathlon-jumping-up-to-scratch-313863.
31. Eleanor Jones, " Major change needed to prevent future pentathlon issues," *Horse and Hound*, August 16, 2021, https://www.horseandhound.co.uk/news/major-change-needed-to-prevent-future-pentathlon-issues-758542
32. Zjan Shirinian, "Extreme heat in Acapulco sees women's pentathlon final stopped," *insidethegames*, April 27, 2021, https://www.insidethegames.biz/articles/1018647/extreme-heat-in-acapulco-sees-women-s-pentathlon-final-stopped.
33. Sandra Heck, "L'institutionnalisation d'une idée. Le pentathlon moderne, du programme olympique à une fédération internationale," *Cahiers de l'INSEP*, no. 46 (2010), 212-214, https://www.persee.fr/doc/insep_1241-0691_2010_num_46_1_1130.
34. Letter, Pierre de Coubertin to Godefroy de Blonay, 20 April 1912, A-PO2-1912-04-20, Manuscripts Pierre de Coubertin, IOC Archive.
35. "UIPM Constitutional Book," *UIPM World Pentathlon*, accessed January 27, 2022, https://www.uipmworld.org/sites/default/files/constitutional_book_uipm_2018.pdf.
36. "Member Federations," *UIPM World Pentathlon*, accessed February 6, 2022, https://www.uipmworld.org/member-federations.
 Jens Weinreich, "Black Card für den Modernen Fünfkampf," *Sport & Politics*, August 7, 2021, https://www.jensweinreich.de/2021/08/07/black-card-fuer-den-modernen-fuenfkampf/.
37. "UIPM Official Statement: Horse Welfare and Athlete Safety in Modern Pentathlon," *UIPM World Pentathlon*, August 8, 2021, https://www.uipmworld.org/news/uipm-official-statement-horse-welfare-and-athlete-safety-modern-pentathlon.

The Movement

1. "UIPM Disciplinary Panel: Kim Raisner and Annika Schleu," *UIPM World Pentathlon*, September 6, 2021, https://www.uipmworld.org/news/uipm-disciplinary-panel-kim-raisner-and-annika-schleu-ger.
2. Colm O'Connor, "Modern pentathlon chief blames athletes for horse complaints: 'Everything was genius, was super'," *Irish Examiner*, August 6, 2021, https://www.irishexaminer.com/sport/othersport/arid-40354229.html.
3. See for example: *Lincoln Allison and Alan Tomlinson, Understanding International Sport Organisations: Principles, Power and Possibilities* (London: Routledge, 2017).
4. Elaine (@LittleWhtBlouse), "Imagine what she does to the horse when no one's watching." *Twitter*, August 7, 2021, https://twitter.com/LittleWhtBlouse/status/1423951504080351240.
5. "Pferdemisshandlung bei Olympia: Deutscher Tierschutzbund stellt Strafanzeige gegen Trainerin und Reiterin," *Deutscher Tierschutzbund e.V.*, August 13, 2021, https://www.tierschutzbund.de/news-storage/heimtiere/130821-pferdemisshandlung-bei-olympia-deutscher-tierschutzbund-stellt-strafanzeige-gegen-trainerin-und-reiterin/.
6. "Moderner Fümfkampf - Tokio 2020 - Verfahren wegen Tierquälerei eingestellt," *ZDF*, January 11, 2021,https://www.zdf.de/nachrichten/sport/moderner-fuenfkampf-schleu-raisner-olympia-reiten-pferd-verfahren-tierquaelerei-100.html.
7. Klaus Schormann, "Klaus Schormann: UIPM has been proactive on horse welfare as wheel keeps on turning toward Paris 2024," *insidethegames*, September 25, 2021, https://www.insidethegames.biz/articles/1113412/blog-klaus-schormann.
8. "UIPM Official Statement: Horse Welfare and Athlete Safety in Modern Pentathlon," UIPM World Pentathlon, August 8, 2021, https://www.uipmworld.org/news/uipm-official-statement-horse-welfare-and-athlete-safety-modern-pentathlon.
9. Ibid.
10. "UIPM Forms Riding Working Group and Appoints Disciplinary Panel," *UIPM World Pentathlon*, August 20, 2021, https://www.uipmworld.org/news/uipm-forms-riding-working-group-and-appoints-disciplinary-panel.
11. Ibid.
12. "UIPM President's Activities: September/October 2021," *UIPM World Pentathlon*, November 9, 2021, https://www.uipmworld.org/news/uipm-presidents-activities-septemberoctober-2021.
13. UIPM, "2021 UIPM Congress Working Document," Monaco, November 27-28, 2021, 197.
14. Jens Weinreich, "Der Dauerkampf des Klaus Schormann," *Spiegel*, December 10, 2021, (https://www.spiegel.de/sport/moderner-fuenfkampf-bei-olympia-klaur-schormann-und-sein-dauerkampf-a-3caea1cd-f01a-4279-b574-27c203aec8e8.
15. Antoine Huot de Saint Albin, "Pourquoi ça chauffe au pentathlon moderne après la suppression de l'équitation," *20 minutes*, December 3, 2021, https://www.20minutes.fr/sport/3187095-20211203-jo-pourquoi-ca-chauffe-pentathlon-moderne-apres-suppression-equitation.
16. UIPM, "CAPM 2021 Congress Minutes," online, November 10, 2021, 2.
17. "Open Letter to Pentathletes," *UIPM World Pentathlon*, November 4, 2021, https://www.uipmworld.org/news/open-letter-pentathletes.
18. UIPM, "UIPM 2021 Congress Minutes," Monaco/online, November 27-28, 2021, 15.
19. "LA28 Initial Sports Programme to be put forward to the IOC Session," *International Olympic Committee*, December 9, 2021, https://olympics.com/ioc/news/la28-initial-sports-programme-to-be-put-forward-to-the-ioc-session.

20. Liam Morgan, "Skateboarding, surfing and sport climbing proposed for inclusion at Los Angeles 2028," *insidethegames*, December 9, 2021, https://www.insidethegames.biz/articles/1116604/ioc-los-angeles-2028-programme-sports.
21. "UIPM New 5th Discipline Working Group Enjoy Hugely Productive First Meeting," UIPM World Pentathlon, January 18, 2022, "https://www.uipmworld.org/news/uipm-new-5th-discipline-working-group-enjoy-hugely-productive-first-meeting.
22. James M. Jasper, "Emotions and social movements: Twenty years of Theory and Research," *Annual Review of Sociology* 37 (2011): 285-303, https://www.annualreviews.org/doi/pdf/10.1146/annurev-soc-081309-150015.
23. Hannah Borenstein, "On Your Mark."
24. Andrew Dowdeswell, "Exclusive: More than 650 modern pentathletes issue vote of no confidence in UIPM President Schormann," *insidethegames*, November 5, 2021, https://www.insidethegames.biz/articles/1115074/modern-pentathlon-uipm-schormann.
25. Joe Choong (@JoeChoongy), "Anyone reading this, our President claims he only recognises 10-15 names on a list of athletes that signed a letter against him. Just goes to show how little the UIPM care about all the athletes, or how well they actually know the sport #savepentathlon," *Twitter*, November 7, 2021, https://twitter.com/JoeChoongy/status/1457123282436726789.
26. Joe Choong (@JoeChoongy), "@olmypics is it true you've asked UIPM to remove horseriding from our sport? #savepentathlon," *Twitter*, November 4, 2021, https://twitter.com/JoeChoongy/status/1456295402613919750.
27. Mike Rowbottom, "Dozens of Olympic medalists ask IOC President to prevent UIPM removing riding from modern pentathlon programme," *insidethegames*, November 5, 2021, https://www.insidethegames.biz/articles/1115905/uipm-riding-ioc-bach-letter-olympic-list.
28. Pierre de Coubertin, "Olympic Letter XVI," in *Olympism. Selected Writings*, ed. Norbert Müller (Lausanne: International Olympic Committee, 2000): 178.
29. "Natsu Ohta," *UIPM World Pentathlon*, accessed February 2, 2022, https://www.uipmworld.org/athlete/natsu-ohta.
30. Mike Rowbottom, "French wins women's UIPM World Cup as 13-year-old Ohta suffers riding fall," *insidethegames*, March 26, 2021, https://www.insidethegames.biz/articles/1105921/french-ohta-uipm-world-cup-budapest.
31. Samuel Benton, "New off the blocks," *Australasian Leisure Management* 133 (March 2019): 14-15, https://search.informit.org/doi/abs/10.3316/informit.500450046869322.
32. Michael Pavitt, "Denmark calls for UIPM to rescind "unlawful" decision to drop riding discipline for Los Angeles 2028," *insidethegames*, November 11, 2021, https://www.insidethegames.biz/articles/1115312/denmark-uipm-riding-modern-pentathlon.
33. "About," *Pentathlon United*, accessed March 11, 2022, https://pentathlonunited.com.
34. "Save Modern Pentathlon," *gofundme*, accessed February 2, 2022, https://www.gofundme.com/f/save-modern-pentathlon?qid=7b1bcb74e55e3880487a53792181f759.
35. Grit Hartmann, "Tipping the Scales of Justice - The Sport and Its "Supreme Courts,"" *Play The Game*, accessed January 28, 2022, https://www.playthegame.org/media/10851569/Tipping-the-scales-of-justice---the-sport-and-its-supreme-court.pdf.
36. Helen Lenskyj, "Sport exceptionalism and the Court of Arbitration for Sport," *Journal of Criminological Research Policy and Practice* 4, no. 1 (2018): 5-17, https://doi.org/10.1108/JCRPP-01-2018-0002.
37. Grit Hartmann, "Tipping the Scales of Justice."
38. Arnout Geeraert, "Theoretical framework: three models of democracy," in *Strengthening Athlete Power in Sport*, ed. Mike McNamee (Aarhus: Play The Game, 2021): 9-13, https://www.playthegame.org/media/10753881/Strengthening-Athlete-Power-in-Sport_lit-review.pdf.
39. Ibid.
40. Johannes Klamet, "Athleten Deutschland e.V. - From founding to funding," (Master

Oppression of Athletes' Voices

1. Seltmann, "The Institutional Position of Athletes."
2. Letter, Athletes and coaches of pentathlon family to Klaus Schormann, "RE proposed combined event; shooting and running," April 14, 2007.
3. Letter, Klaus Schormann to Stefano Giommoni, "RE: letter received regarding combined shooting running event," June 10, 2007.
4. UIPM, "UIPM 2021 Congress Minutes."
5. "Open Letter to Pentathletes," *UIPM World Pentathlon*.
6. Andrew Dowdeswell, "Exclusive: Schmitt slams Schormann and UIPM, claims removal of riding unconstitutional," *insidethegames*, November 17, 2021, https://www.insidethegames.biz/articles/1115563/schmitt-schormann-uipm-modern-pentathlon.
7. Lenskyj, *The Olympic Games*, 109.
8. Though this cannot be verified because the minutes of this meeting are not publicly available.
9. Pentathlon United (@PentUnited), "Athletes have been sending their opinions to the @WorldPentathlon athletes' committee over the last few days. Now it's time for us to hear what we've all been saying, and find out how the athlete representative will vote at congress #savepentathlon #pentathlonunited," *Twitter*, November 26, 2021, https://twitter.com/PentUnited/status/1464366596005183492/photo/1.
10. UIPM, "UIPM 2021 Congress Minutes," 12.
11. "UIPM New 5th Discipline Working Group Enjoys Hugely Productive Meeting," *UIPM World Pentathlon*, January 22, 2022, https://www.uipmworld.org/news/uipm-new-5th-discipline-working-group-enjoy-hugely-productive-first-meeting.
12. Pentathlon United (@PentUnited), "This man, @WorldPentathlon treasurer, and one of many like minded "leaders," making a joke about being an athlete, thinking he represents our views. Now our sport is potentially out of the Olympic Program #SavePentathlon #PentathlonUnited @Olympics #KlausOut #ModernPentathlon," *Twitter*, December 9, 2021, https://twitter.com/PentUnited/status/1469057748109254659.
13. This was mentioned by an interviewee who was present at the meeting.
14. Han Xiao, "Athletes First?: The Right to Health and Safety in Postponing the Tokyo Olympic Games," *Human Rights Defender* 29, no. 2 (August 2020): 19-21.
15. Peak Pentathlon (@peakpentathlon), "Survey results by USAPM Athlete representatives. Despite overwhelming* athlete, coach, and parent support of keeping riding and a vote of no confidence in UIPM, USAPM still released a statement supporting the removal of riding AND voted support the UIPM EB's motion to remove riding. If you do not represent your athletes, coaches, or parents, who do you present @usapentathlonmultisport? *undecided means neither yes nor no* #savepentathlon #KeepTheHorses #ModernPentathlon #UIPMriding," *Instagram*, December 2, 2021, https://www.instagram.com/p/CW_u0zPpDNo/.
16. Peak Pentathlon (@peakpentathlon), "More secret meetings and a further disregard for their athletes' voices. After receiving a petition with 252 signatures and letter with 54 athletes' signatures (majority), USAPM leadership proceeded to ignore its athletes voices to reject UIPM's unlawful decision to remove riding despite the function of the Board to be to represent its community and athletes per Section 7.2 of its bylaws. #savepentathlon #KeepTheHorses #ModernPentathlon #UIPMriding," Instagram, November 21, 2021, https://www.instagram.com/p/CWxLRawM4lq/.
17. Ibid.

18. Pentathlon United (@PentUnited), "This man, @WorldPentathlon treasurer."
19. Jens Alm, ed., Action for *Good Governance in International Sports Organisations* (Copenhagen: Playthegame, 2013), https://www.playthegame.org/knowledge-bank/downloads/action-for-good-governance-in-international-sports-organisations-final-report/38a18089-001b-4b8e-8ace-ac0500d654db.

Disregard for Principles of Governance

1. Jens Alm, *Sports Governance Observer* 2019 (Aarhus: Play The Game, 2019), https://www.playthegame.org/theme-pages/the-sports-governance-observer/.
2. Arnout Geeraert, "Measuring governance: the Sports Governance Observer," in *Research Handbook on Sport Governance*, ed. Mathieu Winand and Christos Anagnostopoulos (Cheltenham: Edward Elgar, 2019): 29-52, https://doi.org/10.4337/9781786434821.000 09.
3. Arnout Geeraert, *Sports Governance Observer* 2018. An assessment of good governance in five international sports federations (Aarhus: Play The Game, 2018), https://playthegame.org/knowledge-bank/downloads/sports-governance-observer-2018/205c4aa7-4036-4fe1-b570-a99601700e5d.
4. Sunder Katwala, *Democratising Global Sport* (London: Foreign Policy Center, 2000), 27.
5. Nick Butler, "Exclusive: Ricci Bitti outlines importance of term limits for International Federation Presidents," *insidethegames*, July 8, 2017, https://www.insidethegames.biz/articles/1052455/exclusive-ricci-bitti-outlines-importance-of-term-limits-for-international-federation-presidents.
6. Alm, ed., *Action for Good Governance*, 190.
7. See for example: Lincoln Allison and Alan Tomlinson, *Understanding International Sport Organisations*.
8. Jens Weinreich, "Programmhinweis: Sportgespräch mit dem Überlebenskünstler Klaus Schormann, Präsident des Weltverbandes der Modernen Fünfkämpfer (UIPM)," *Sport & Politics*, August 17, 2012, https://www.jensweinreich.de/2012/08/17/programmhinweis-sportgesprach-mit-dem-uberlebenskunstler-klaus-schormann-prasident-des-weltverbandes-der-modernen-funfkampfer-uipm/.
9. UIPM, *Modern pentathlon 50 anniversary*, UIPM, 1999, Stark Center for Physical Culture and Sports at the University of Texas at Austin.
10. He is the son of former IOC President Juan Antonio Samaranch.
11. Alm, ed., *Action for Good Governance*, 210.
12. Allison and Tomlinson, *Understanding International Sport Organisations*, 218.
13. Ibid.
14. Klaus Schormann, "Sitzen Sie Bequem? Klaus Schormann," interview by Jens Weinreich, Sport & Politics, August 17, 2012, audio, 3:30, https://www.jensweinreich.de/wp-content/audio/Sitzen%20Sie%20Bequem%201%20Klaus%20Schormann%20 17082012.mp3.
15. Huot de Saint Albin, "Pourquoi ça."
16. Andrew Dowdeswell, "Exclusive: UIPM denies using delay tactics as MPADK told riding appeal must go to UIPM Court of Arbitration before the CAS," *insidethegames*, November 23, 2021, https://www.insidethegames.biz/articles/1115842/uipm-modern-pentathlon-cas-denmark.
17. ASOIF Governance Support and Monitoring Unit, "Guidance notes for IFs considering holding virtual General Assemblies," *ASOIF*, accessed January 28, 2022, https://www.asoif.com/sites/default/files/download/asoif_gsmu_-_guidance_notes_for_ifs_consider-

ing_holding_virtual_general_assemblies_-_3_dec.pdf.
18. Allison and Tomlinson, *Understanding International Sport Organisations*.
19. "Clientelism," in *Encyclopedia of Social Measurement*, accessed February 2, 2022, https://www.sciencedirect.com/topics/social-sciences/clientelism.
20. Peter Forsberg, *A Vote With A Weight. An analysis of alternatives to the one-nation-one-vote system in international sport* (Aarhus: Play The Game, 2022), https://www.playthegame.org/media/10969676/A-vote-with-a-weight_final.pdf.
21. Jürgen Mittag, "Sport and the one-nation-one-vote system," interview by Play The Game, *Play The Game*, April 5, 2013, text, https://www.playthegame.org/news/news-articles/2013/sport-and-the-one-nation-one-vote-system/.
22. Schormann, "Sitzen Sie Bequem?"
23. Namibia did not participate in the voting at the 2021 General Assembly.
24. "UIPM Receives Official Support from National Governing Bodies on 5th Discipline Consultation," *UIPM World Pentathlon*, November 18, 2021, https://www.uipmworld.org/news/uipm-receives-official-support-national-governing-bodies-5th-discipline-consultation.
25. Forwarded email to the author, December 19, 2021.
26. UIPM, "2021 UIPM Congress Working Document," 41
27. John Sugden and Alan Tomlinson, *FIFA and the Contest for World Football and Great Balls of Fire: How Big Money is Hijacking World Football* (Edinburgh and London: Mainstream, 1999); Jörg Krieger, *Power and Politics in World Athletics. A Critical History* (London: Routledge, 2021).
28. Jeppe L. Brock, Henrik B. Jacobsen, and Christian Heide-Jørgensen, "Papua Ny Guinea: 'Håndbold var ikke en sport her, før IHF kontaktede os'," *Politiken*, December 17, 2015, https://politiken.dk/sport/haandbold/art5603050/Papua-Ny-Guinea-»Håndbold-var-ikke-en-sport-her-før-IHF-kontaktede-os.
29. Eleonora Ottaviani, "FEI General Assembly, Antwerp: Food For Thought," *International Jumping Riders Club*, n.d., https://www.ijrc.org/en/News-results-1/FEI-General-Assembly-Antwerp-Food-for-thought.html.
30. Forsberg, *A Vote With A Weight*.
31. Huot de Saint Albin, "Pourquoi ça."
32. UIPM, "UIPM 2021 Congress Minutes," 11.
33. "Moderner Fünfkampf - Radsport wird nicht die neue Sportart," *Sportschau*, November 7, 2021, https://www.sportschau.de/moderner-fuenfkampf/moderner-fuenfkampf-106.html.
34. Liam Morgan, "UIPM denies decision made on riding replacement as athletes invited to Executive Board call," *insidethegames*, November 8, 2021, https://www.insidethegames.biz/articles/1115179/uipm-denies-decision-made-fifth-sport.
35. James Ayles, "Spartan Race Targets Further Global Expansion And Olympic Recognition After Successful 2019 Season Ends With First-Ever Obstacle Course Race Held At Twickenham," *Forbes*, December 5, 2019, https://www.forbes.com/sites/jamesayles/2019/12/05/spartan-race-targets-further-global-expansion-and-olympic-recognition-after-successful-2019-season-ends-with-first-ever-obstacle-course-race-held-at-twickenham/.
36. Mike Rowbottom, "Exclusive: Former world champion Tymoshchenko claims new UIPM discipline will involve obstacle racing," *insidethegames*, December 24, 2021, https://www.insidethegames.biz/articles/1117224/uipm-modern-pentathlon-obstacle-racinghttps://www.insidethegames.biz/articles/1117224/uipm-modern-pentathlon-obstacle-racing.
37. "UIPM Newsletter May/June 2016," *UIPM World Pentathlon*, accessed January 22, 2022, http://www.pentathlon.org/wp-content/uploads/UIPM_Newsletter_May_June_2016.pdf.
38. "UIPM New Executive Board Meeting: Samaranch Jr Elected First Vice-President,"

UIPM World Pentathlon, January 21, 2017, https://www.uipmworld.org/news/uipm-new-executive-board-meeting-samaranch-jr-elected-1st-vice-president.
39. "UIPM Laser-Run with Obstacles Is Born With Los Angeles Event," *UIPM World Pentathlon*, March 1, 2017, https://www.uipmworld.org/printpdf/news-page/106290.
40. "Joe De Sena Has Olympic Dreams For Obstacle Racing," *Vermont Sports*, September 6, 2016, https://vtsports.com/joe-de-sena-has-olympic-dreams-for-obstacle-racing/.
41. "UIPM New Executive Board Meeting," *UIPM World Pentathlon*, January 21, 2017.
42. Dumitru Cătălin Cohal, "The History of Pentathlon Competitions," *International Conference Knowledge-Based Organization* 25, no. 2 (2019): 234-239, https://doi.org/10.2478/kbo-2019-0087.
43. Geeraert, *Sports Governance Observer* 2018.
44. Mittag, "Sport and the one-nation-one-vote system."
45. UIPM score: 43,8%; the average mean of all assessed IFs at the time was 49,6%.
46. See discussions here: "Special Edition: Refuting IOC's Plan," *The Sport Journal*.
47. Heck, "Modern Pentathlon at the 2012 London Olympics."
48. Ibid.
49. Belinda Wheaton, and Holly Thorpe, "Action Sport Media Consumption Trends Across Generations: Exploring the Olympic Audience and the Impact of Action Sports Inclusion," *Communication & Sport* 7, no. 4 (2019): 415-445, https://doi.org/10.1177/2167479518780410.
50. "IOC Executive Board addresses situation of International Weightlifting Federation," *International Olympic Committee*, October 7, 2020, https://olympics.com/ioc/news/ioc-executive-board-addresses-situation-of-international-weightlifting-federation.
51. Seltmann, "Disrupting institutional reproduction?."
52. Andrew Dowdeswell, "Modern pentathletes unite to challenge UIPM on riding decision before Executive Board call," *insidethegames*, November 12, 2021, https://www.insidethegames.biz/articles/1115360/modern-pentathlon-uipm-riding-board.
53. Forwarded email to the author, December 24, 2021.
54. UIPM, "UIPM 2021 Congress Minutes," 10.
55. Forwarded email to the author, December 20, 2021.
56. "UIPM Official Statement: 5th Discipline Consultation, IOC Executive Board," *UIPM World Pentathlon*, December 9, 2021, https://www.uipmworld.org/news/uipm-official-statement-5th-discipline-consultation-ioc-executive-board.
57. Ibid.
58. Andrew Dowdeswell, "Exclusive: Schmitt slams Schormann and UIPM, claims removal of riding unconstitutional," *insidethegames*, November 17, 2021, https://www.insidethegames.biz/articles/1115563/schmitt-schormann-uipm-modern-pentathlon.
59. See for example: Jens Alm, *Sports Governance Observer 2019. An assessment of good governance in six international sports federations* (Aarhus: Play The Game, 2019), https://www.playthegame.org/knowledge-bank/downloads/sports-governance-observer-2019/275a52c3-c8a0-4a85-8b8f-aae2008a03c1.

Conclusion: The Big Picture and Wider Implications

1. Helen Lenskyj, "Let the Games Begin?."
2. Dave Zirin and Jules Boykoff, "Olympic Athletes Deserve Freedom of Speech," *The Nation*, July 8, 2021, https://www.thenation.com/article/society/olympic-athletes-deserve-freedom-of-speech/.
3. Jasper, Protest: A Cultural Introduction.
4. "UIPM New 5th Discipline Working Group," *UIPM World Pentathlon*, January 18, 2022.

5. John Sugden and Alan Tomlinson, "Digging the Dirt and Staying Clean."
6. See also my response to the reviewers at the beginning of this book.
7. McDonald, "Critical social research," 107.

Afterword: Response to Reviewers

1. Haack, Susan, "Peer Review and Publication: Lessons for Lawyers," *Stetson Law Review* 36, no. 3 (2007): 789-819, https://ssrn.com/abstract=1089072.
2. Richard Smith, "Opening up BMJ peer review: A beginning that should lead to complete transparency," *British Medical Journal* 318 (January 1999): 4-5, https://doi.org/10.1136/bmj.318.7175.4.
3. Richard Smith, "Peer review: flawed process at the heart of science and journals," *Journal of the Royal Society of Medicine* 99, no. 4 (2006): 178-182, https://doi.org/10.1258/jrsm.99.4.178.
4. Michael J. Mahoney, "Publication Prejudices: An Experimental Study of Confirmatory Bias in the Peer Review System," *Cognitive Therapy and Research* 1, no. 2 (1977): 161-175, https://doi.org/10.1007/BF01173636.
5. Gwen Ottinger, "Is it good science? Activism, values, and communicating politically relevant science," *Journal of Science Communication* 14, no. 2 (2015), C02.
6. Lara Drew and Nik Taylor, "Engaged Activist Research: A Challenge to Apolitical Objectivity," in *Defining Critical Animal Studies: An Intersectional Social Justice Approach for Liberation*, ed. Anthony J. Nocella II, John Sorenson, Kim Socha, and Atsuko Matsuoko (New York: Peter Lang, 2014), 158-176.
7. Paul Dimeo, *A History of Drug Use in Sport: 1876 - 1976: Beyond Good and Evil* (London: Routledge, 2007).
8. Thomas M. Hunt, Drug Games. *The International Olympic Committee and the Politics of Doping, 1960–2008* (Austin: University of Texas Press, 2011).
9. Verner Møller, *The Scapegoat – about the expulsion of Michael Rasmussen from the Tour de France 2007 and beyond* (People's Press: Copenhagen, 2011).
10. Michel-Rolph Trouillot, *Silencing the Past* (Boston: Beacon Press, 2015).
11. Ben Jones, "Political Activism and Research Ethics," *Journal of Applied Philosophy* 37, no. 2 (2019): 233-248. https://doi.org/10.1111/japp.12366.
12. C. Wright Mills, *The Sociological Imagination* (Oxford: Oxford University Press, 2000).

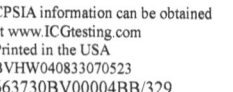
CPSIA information can be obtained
at www.ICGtesting.com
Printed in the USA
BVHW040833070523
663730BV00004BB/329